STORIES OF OTHER WORLDS

COLIN EVERARD

In Africa at age 21

In Europe at age 94

THE MARCH OF TIME

STORIES OF OTHER WORLDS

A Collection of the Author's Stories, Including Excerpts of the Author's Published Texts Related to Africa

COLIN EVERARD

Troubador Publishing Ltd
Unit E2 Airfield Business Park
Harrison Road, Market Harborough
Leicestershire LE16 7UL
Tel: 0116 279 2299
Email: books@troubador.co.uk
Web: www.troubador.co.uk

ISBN 978-1-83628-063-7

British Library Cataloguing in Publication Data.
A catalogue record for this book is available from the British Library.

rinted and bound by CPI Group (UK) Ltd, Croydon, CR0 4YY
Typeset in 11pt Aldine by Troubador Publishing Ltd, Leicester, UK

FSC
www.fsc.org
MIX
Paper | Supporting responsible forestry
FSC® C013604

My collection of short stories is dedicated to the memory of my wonderfully perfect wife, Emy.

CONTENTS

ACKNOWLEDGEMENTS

No Man Is An Island
John Donne. 1624

Note: References to Man should be understood to mean Mankind, both sexes.

No man is an island,
Entire of itself;
Every man is a piece of the continent,
A part of the main.
If a clod be washed away by the sea,
Europe is the less.

I believe that, today, John Donne's words are echoed and frequently re–echoed. Increasingly, it seems, on Earth, we rely for our existence on information provided by a specialist, rather than by a generalist. In any case, for many years I have relied on the advice and help of others. Naturally, I am the first to acknowledge their support.

And so it is with the stories in this book – yes, my gratitude is indeed well–earned by those named below.

First and foremost, I wish to acknowledge the tremendous support of my publisher, Troubador Publishing and the

Production Manager, Holly Porter for her meticulous attention to detail and endless patience!

For their continuing readiness to provide essential support in terms of correctness of substance, formatting and so forth, I wish to strongly acknowledge the excellent efforts of Professor Andrea Everard and Professor Anuradha Sivarama; both are of the University of Delaware, USA.

In addition to the invaluable guidance and support of the above–named two professors, I wish to acknowledge with deep gratitude the assistance of several others; the work covered included proofreading, text correcting, formatting, reading texts to me, text review and raising relevant feedback questions, and other necessary associated work.

I shall name some of these individuals now; all of them made important contributions to the preparation of the manuscript. All gave generously of their time; for this, I wish here and now to express my deepest gratitude.

My list includes: Mrs. Shirley Palla, Mrs. Halina Biernacki, Dr. Emy Everard, Miss Karin Lunz, Mrs. Maria Lanjus, Miss Polina Jigoulina.

I wish to thank all very sincerely for their encouragement and ready support.

Colin Everard
Vienna. March 2024.

MY LETTER OF INTRODUCTION

Knowledge, Truth, Understanding, Happiness, Patience, Tolerance – These Are Attributes of the Good Life

Dear Reader, thank you for looking at my book; I hope this will become a rewarding experience. You may well wonder why the beginning of the introduction is unorthodox. It is so because from the outset, I would like to regard you as an acquaintance; and I hope that as you progress through the pages which follow, as my acquaintance, you will identify with my experiences, as I recount my Stories of Other Worlds.

En passant, at the same time, one learns about the course of my destiny, which is something, in our individual ways, we have in common; I have no doubt that your destiny is at least as eventful as mine, although almost certainly in different ways. As you share my experiences, I will feel privileged if, by the end of your reading, our acquaintances may develop into friendship, a friendship during which, long after you have closed the covers of my book, you will meditate on what I have conveyed to you; yes, my intention is to give you food for thought. And this food for thought has nothing to do with theories; throughout, we are dealing with real–life experience.

I can well understand an immediate reaction. On what grounds does someone called Colin Everard believe he is properly qualified to embark on telling short stories which, in his opinion, might help the reader better understand her or his perception of one's place in our global community, a community of lands which embrace a myriad of cultures amid widely diverse attitudes of their peoples?

I will confidently respond to this basic question. First, I have visited and closely worked with the peoples of more than fifty countries; and, invariably, I took great interest in the culture and human values of the people with whom I worked. In addition to visiting these countries (some many times), I lived in seven of them for protracted periods. Some of these countries were among the handful of the so–called developed world; others were what are generally described as developing nations. Of the countries where I lived and worked, some were among the poorest in our world; for example, one was Somalia, tragically currently politically disintegrated as a nation, a country with a strong element of anarchy, with its associated terrorism.

En passant, as a foreigner, I became one of a handful who spoke the Somali language fluently, with perfect pronunciation and the all–important intonation; at that time, most regarded correct pronunciation by a foreigner as virtually impossible, partly due to the guttural speech element.

Along the way of my professional experience, as I was pulled up the work ladder, sometimes my colleagues would describe me and my approach to the challenging tasks which lay ahead of us as a practical and practicing attitude of idealism.

I am beginning to hope that, with my unusual background and wide experience in many exotic countries, you may soon be convinced that I am adequately qualified to write my short stories; they have been selected from a multitude, from Africa, Asia and Europe.

This is my fifth book; my books include non–fiction and fiction. I wish to emphasise that, regardless of delays, I go to great lengths to assure the correctness and truth of the information I give to my readers. Before I could find time to embark on what it takes to write a book, thirty–four of my articles were published in professional journals; most of the journals were published internationally and my articles were almost always translated into four languages, sometimes six.

As you progress through the pages of this book, please make a strong effort to really understand the implications of the text. However interesting you may find the information provided, information which will often be new to many readers, it is important to meditate on the implications of the stories. By doing this, you will enable me to realise my goal in writing this book.

And what is my goal? It is to make a worthwhile contribution to our understanding of people in other lands, near or far. Once many of us begin to really understand the cultures of our fellow human beings, we will reverse the spiral of the situation in many countries today, where what is accepted as normal in fact bears little or no relationship to what, over millennia, has been developed and generally practised as correct conduct, whether at the domestic, national level or internationally by the world community. We must strive to replace evil and the wretched consequences of evil with goodness and decency. Too often, ignorance, misinformation, threats and the like (for example, the threat of nuclear war) breed misunderstandings, acrimony, anxiety, suspicion, deceit, even hatred. Often, mutual suspicion, or worse, proves to be groundless.

So, each of us could earnestly consider how best to personally participate in initiating the process of consciously, and with all the energy one can muster, taking personal action to regain the upper hand. In this context, one is reminded of an American poet, Josiah Gilbert Holland, who, in the mid nineteenth century, wrote the lines which follow. Although he refers only to 'men', unquestionably the thoughts expressed in his poem should be considered by us all.

GOD, give us men!
A time like this demands
Strong minds, great hearts, true faith and ready hands;
Men whom the lust of office does not kill;
Men whom the spoils of office can not buy;
Men who possess opinions and a will;
Men who have honour; men who will not lie;
Men who can stand before a demagogue
And damn his treacherous flatteries without winking!
Tall men, sun–crowned, who live above the fog
In public duty, and in private thinking;
For while the rabble, with their thumb–worn creeds,
Their large professions and their little deeds,
Mingle in selfish strife, lo! Freedom weeps,
Wrong rules the land and waiting Justice sleeps.

I believe that through a better understanding of cultures and the ways which for our neighbour are her or his norm, this will generate within us understanding, which itself may in turn well lead to a relatively greater degree of tolerance and patience within each of us.

I also believe strongly that we all deserve to live in a world community that is altogether better than is currently the case. We should be freed of the torment which bears down on us in our daily lives. Evil concepts, often with dire, life–threatening consequcnces which are treated today as the routine norm, need objective, in–depth examination, followed by drastic reform. There is not the slightest suggestion from me that we should live in the past – we should always look forward. At the same time, however, we should restore the well–tried, good norms of the past.

This book will be my last. I am already happily preparing for my next world. In the meantime, I invite you, dear Reader, to accompany me on journeys to other worlds. I again ask you to meditate on the substance of my stories. And after you have digested the knowledge contained in the pages which follow, I hope you will have gained more understanding of 'worlds' other than yours. And with this understanding, we should all join the movement to do our personal utmost to bridging the gap between our world and those of others. As we progress in our task, we should spread reason and happiness.

And the ultimate aim of each of us must be to contribute to creating a better world community for us all. Yes, this is a tall order, but with our concerted will, we can make it happen – and why not start today?

Bon Voyage!

Colin Everard
Vienna. 2023

STORIES OF AFRICA

THE HORN OF AFRICA

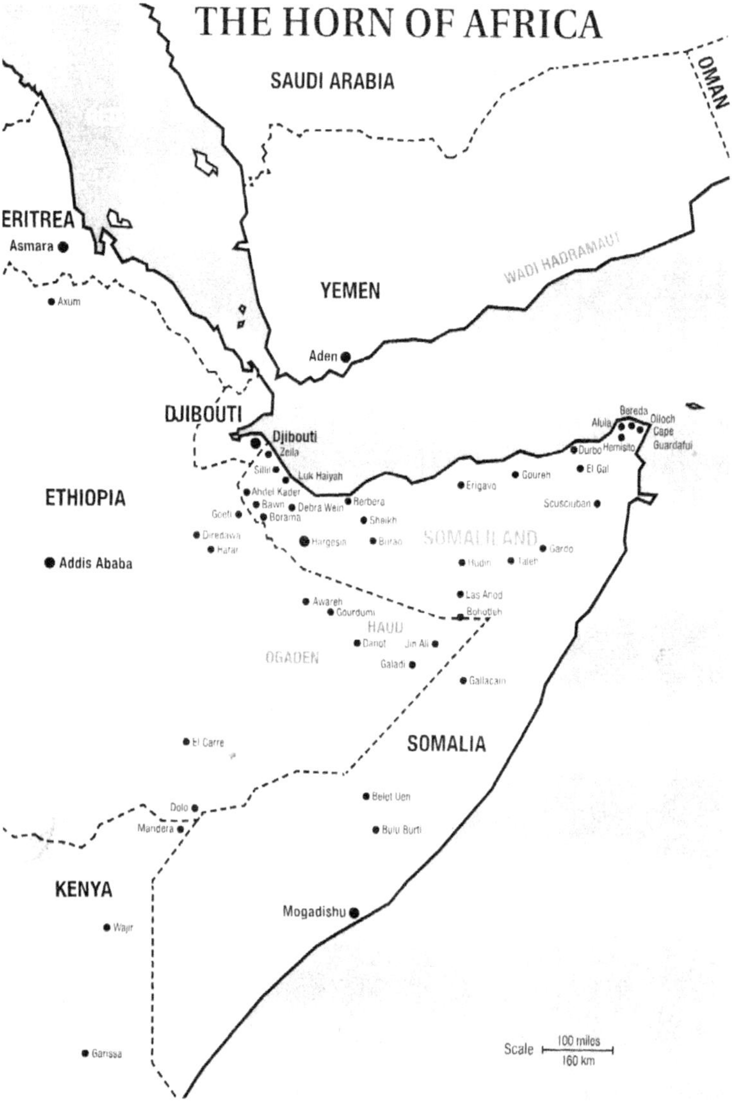

ONE

WHAT IS A DESERT LOCUST?

One way, dear Reader, to describe the desert locust is to share with you my own experience concerning how I first became aware of this insect.

In 1949, I encountered the desert locust somewhat coincidentally. I had been conscripted for military service and, after a few weeks undergoing training, I was selected for further training so as to become a commissioned officer. I then found myself designated as a 'Z' man; this meant I was included, along with thousands of others, as an officer to receive special training to fight in the Korean War, which would begin in the following year.

In fact, I was not despatched to Korea; instead, with three fellow officers, I was sent for military duty to the then Somaliland Protectorate, a small country in the Horn of Africa.

There, I became a member of the Somali Scouts, a force which was not only responsible for defending the border of the country, but also was used to help maintain relative peace in areas adjacent to the border; these areas were often populated by anarchic, armed tribesmen who were, in fact, bandits. Especially during periods of drought, there were almost daily armed skirmishes to gain control of valuable watering holes, which were needed by different clans to water their livestock, of mainly camels and cattle.

I was sent on detachment to such areas to intervene between the warring parties and establish co–existence between the opposing sides. This role was difficult and dangerous, since the bandits used to shoot to kill. Although as a boy I had been conditioned to scenes of death during the Second World War (WW2 had ended in May 1945), I was nevertheless sometimes deeply shocked by the scenes of mortality I was forced to witness. For example, on one occasion, I counted at least eighty corpses, some of which were horribly bloody.

After a few months, I was recalled to the military headquarters, based in the main town, Hargeisa. There, I was asked to assist with administrative duties.

During this period, while sleeping peacefully under the open stars, a lion threw me from my bed one night. This was a traumatic experience and, shaken, obviously I was fortunate to have survived.

In retrospect, I've condensed these events for a specific reason. One day, I was asked to attend a meeting with the commanding officer. The decision he would take may well have been influenced by the reports he would have received covering my challenging experiences. In any case, the effect of his decision would strongly impact my destiny.

Colonel Humphrey French was respected and liked. He usually looked relaxed and was quietly assured in his role of commanding officer. "Ah," he said, as I stood at the open door of his office, "always good to see you, Colin – good you survived the *shifta* – the blood–thirsty bandits. You know, you already have a reputation around here; people call you The Lion Man!" The colonel chuckled and gave me a faint smile.

"O.K.," he continued, "we are both busy. So let me get straight to the point. I asked you to join me today because a couple of days ago I received a letter from the government here. They are facing a severe situation – a locust swarm invasion – being one of the sort of thing we Europeans would never think about. According to them, Somali people are risking their entire agriculture, what is apparently going to be a potential catastrophe. They've requested our assistance with one of our officers, and the assignment duration would be about two months."

There then ensued a pause of seconds; Colonel French simply looked at me for another few seconds. With a rather grave countenance, and still staring at me, he went on, "Colin, have you understood everything I have explained to you so far?"

"Yes, sir, everything!" I responded.

"Good. Now you will learn why you are sitting in front of me." As though the Colonel had put his decision behind him, his facial expression suddenly seemed less serious.

"Colin," he said, with a voice that was altogether more relaxed, "you know, I never take a decision lightly. I always try to consider every possible aspect that may result from my decision. And when I have reached a decision, then I put it behind me – and I relax." Now Colonel French was smiling at me; and yes, he was entirely relaxed.

"Although there are a number of your colleagues who are older, with longer overall experience than you, I have decided I will offer you to the government of Somaliland to help cope with the dangerous impending invasion, with its potential catastrophic consequences. Of all the aspects I considered before reaching a decision, there were two important points I will now explain to you.

"First, I have been impressed with the way you handled the situation when you were on detachment. I really doubt that even a more experienced, older man could have done better. So, although you have only recently joined us and you are nineteen years old, it is evident you have qualities of someone well beyond your age." Feeling now altogether more comfortable in front of my commanding officer, it seemed to be my turn to look directly at my Colonel's face. This was a face that expressed not only assured authority, but also benevolence, with a streak bordering on fatherliness.

The Colonel continued, "I firmly believe that good young officers, like you, Colin, should be given every opportunity to expand their horizons. So, in your new assignment, don't just hang around waiting to be told what to do. Get involved, show sensible initiative, and try and get to know the workers – and, if possible, key management staff. You never know, Colin, one of these days these contacts might come in useful. Do you understand, and will you take my advice, Colin?"

"Of course, Colonel; and I appreciate all your good advice. I would like to thank you for your praise and for your confidence in me. On this assignment, I will do my very best! Thank you, Colonel French, for your praise and confidence in me."

"Fine," the colonel said, 'briefly, my second point is that you definitely need a change, after your recent stresses and strains; they take a toll on the system. The change can only do you good.'

The Colonel stood up; so, I followed suit. With a fatherly, gentle smile, he shook my hand and said, "At eight o'clock tomorrow morning, go to the government secretariat and ask for Mr. Gerald Selby–Lowndes. He will be expecting you. Godspeed!"

The next day I was outside the colonel's office, alone – and with a feeling of excited anticipation!

"Ah! You must be Colin Everard – great to meet you." Gerald Selby–Lowndes shook my hand and gestured to a chair. Then he sat next to me "Apart from the time we spend today together, as far as I know. We should work together for the period of your assignment with us. Our organisation is called Desert Locust Control – most people call us DLC. In fact, we started as a scientific research set–up a couple of years ago; it was called Desert Locust Survey, DLS. Now that this whole geographical area will become intensively, and terribly, affected by a vast desert locust plague, the DLC side will become pretty big."

As I was trying to comprehend what my neighbour was explaining to me, I found myself wondering who, in fact, was talking to me.

Gerald Selby–Lowndes was tall, and he had a slim body. He was scantily dressed in khaki shorts and sandals; his upper body, which was a deep brown, was partly covered by a chequered shirt. I judged his age to be about thirty–five years.

As a person, Gerald was well spoken, lucid and invariably

The desert locust (schistocerca gregaria). Some fifty countries are vulnerable to desert locust plagues.

courteous, with charm, and he smiled easily. We soon became good colleagues and firm friends. Unfortunately, our friendship was short-lived; Gerald lost his life by drowning in a sudden flood. I subsequently looked into his background. Gerald's family has retained a notable, positive name in England since the 1200s, having been involved in many national activities, including politics in the eighteenth and nineteenth centuries.

"Right! OK, Colin, now it's time for me to talk, and for you to carefully listen, please." Now the quietly relayed Gerald had quite suddenly become livelier and very much focussed. Then came a question, "Do you know what a desert locust is, and have you read about, or heard of, the accounts of the plagues of Egypt, for example the biblical accounts of antiquity, from 13,000B.C.?"

I responded, "No, Gerald, I know nothing about the desert locust; yes, I have heard of the plagues" of Egypt, but only superficially."

I noticed that Gerald was shuffling a few sheets of photos and diagrams which were lying in front of him. "Good, now I know where to start." Gerald chuckled. "Right at thee beginning!" Handing me a pad, so I could make notes, Gerald spoke.

"The desert locust is a grasshopper, one species of nanny (many?). Its scientific name is *shistocerca gregaria*. The desert locust has several unique characteristics; combined, these make the desert locust the most dangerous migratory pest known to mankind.

"In the 1920s, Sir Boris Uvarov, a brilliant Russian scientist who settled in England, made groundbreaking discoveries relating to locust behaviour and his book *Grasshoppers and Locusts* shed a critical light on previously unknown knowledge of locust behaviour. As a digression, because Uvarov left Russia at about the time of the Revolution, most people thought that the reason why he left Russia was the Revolution. However, this information is incorrect. Being a person of curiosity and initiative, he had started his scientific work, I believe, in Moscow; then he became interested in the possibility of continuing his research work in St. Petersburg and it was after a period in St. Petersburg, during which he had made scientific contacts in Europe and England, he decided that he should further constructively pursue his research in England.

"In England, Uvarov developed his phase theory that, under certain environmental conditions, solitary locusts breed and their offspring behave in a gregarious manner. Since antiquity, no one had even considered the possibility that the locust could change from a solitary to a gregarious state. In other words, everyone thought that the solitary and gregarious grasshopper were, in fact, two separate grasshoppers; so, it was only Uvarov who from his experiments, discovered that the so–called 'two grasshoppers' were one and the same. One could, even today, consider that his amazing research was a sort of revolution in the world of the desert locust.

"The gregarious locusts form swarms which, in turn, cause devastating damage to crop and grassland. In a number of countries, the ravaging locust eats entire crops and, in consequence, people may starve to death. Some of these starving people hang themselves on trees, a quick death being the preferred option.

"The adult female desert locust weights about three grams and the males a bit less than two grams, measuring 3 inches in length (7.5 centimetres). In still air, a locust flies at 12 miles per hour. With a monsoon wind of, say, 40 mph, a locust swarm may travel two hundred miles or more in one day, devouring crops and grazing along the way. Because the monsoon winds bring precipitation, the female locusts find soft sand or loam, into which they can lay their egg pods. Typically, a female lays three times, usually at intervals of several days. On average, each egg pod contains 80 eggs. It goes without saying, therefore, that the generation multiplication rate is colossal.

"Once the female has completed her egg–laying cycle, she dies. Depending on the temperature and humidity in the sand or soft loam, the eggs which have been deposited in pods may remain underground for one or two weeks, sometimes even longer. For the control person, egg fields become visible to the practiced eye; also, local locust scouts are employed to search for egg fields and report on their extent. They may dig up some pods to gauge when the eggs might hatch.

"When the eggs hatch, the nymphs, which are commonly called 'hoppers', force their way to the surface and collect into hopping bands. This stage is called the 'First Instar'. The hoppers shed their skins after about a week, progressing then into the 'Second Instar'. There are five Instars in all, with the hoppers shedding their skins to progress to the next Instar. Once the third Instar is reached, the hoppers organize themselves into large bands and they march in swaths across the terrain, eating the vegetation as they march. In the fourth Instar, the hopper develops wing buds; these become fully developed when the fifth Instar is completed, and such hoppers eat their own weight in food daily. Next one sees a fully developed adult locust, which is pink in colour.

"Left in their natural state, the young locust adults become increasingly active as the days pass. The locusts are already ravenous and fly at a low level in thick, concentrated clusters looking to devour every form of vegetation. Then, after a week or ten days, quite suddenly, the locusts form a swarm, perhaps several square miles in extent. As though a horn has been sounded, at a given moment, the millions of locusts rise as a huge swarm into the air. Now the swarm is on the move, usually carried by a strong monsoon wind. In order to survive, the female adult locust needs to eat at least half of its own weight in food every day. Especially when the swarm comes to roost at twilight, every possible form of vegetation is devoured. Typically, one swarm will eat thirty or forty thousand tons of food every day.

"Obviously, the size and density of swarms vary. However, as an order of magnitude, an average swarm density equates to about fifteen million locusts per square mile. So, when one takes into account the huge multiplication in numbers resulting from breeding, then the number of locusts on the move becomes astronomical.

"Africa had as its main aim the detection of locust egg fields in the Horn of Africa; the application of this strategy extended westwards through Ethiopia and southwards to northern Kenya. Provided sufficient information could be gathered on the movements and breeding of locusts, then a campaign could be planned and launched to destroy the locust nymphs (the hoppers) before they matured into young, flying locusts. So once a locust campaign began, some six or seven weeks would elapse before the so–called 'escape' of the surviving locusts would take place. If the campaign was successful, the escape would be relatively small and many of the surviving locusts would be eaten by predators, mainly birds; others would die through the effect of adverse weather conditions.

"The tactics used to give effect to the strategy involved the positioning of locust control officers to take responsibility for the surveillance and control of locusts within a given geographical area. Provided the locust campaigns were successful, then not only would grazing for nomadic Somalis be preserved, but also significant crops throughout Ethiopia, southern Somalia, and throughout Kenya, Uganda and Tanzania would be saved from destruction.

"If, for some reason, the new generation of locusts escaped from the northern areas on a large scale, then crops and grassland (for livestock) throughout eastern Africa could be destroyed. Many in East Africa recalled devastating invasions of locusts in the 1930s and 1940s. They related how dense locust swarms totally blocked the light of the sun. The railway system became paralysed due to spinning locomotive wheels; squelching locusts nullified the contact between the wheels and the rails.

"In the 1950s, the control of locusts functioned entirely on the ground. The method used to kill the hoppers and young locusts was to spread a mixture of bran and poison ahead of the marching bands of hoppers. The ravenous hoppers were attracted to the bran, ate it – and died of stomach poisoning. It was of obvious importance that the bait used would virtually kill only the hoppers. So, the mixture was about 99% bran and a maximum of 1% poison. The main chemical used was Agrocide also known as Lindane, which was developed and manufactured by Imperial Chemical Industries. Another chemical used was Dieldrin, produced by the Shell Company.

"Although in the Horn of Africa we are certainly one of the most important geographical areas regarding invasions of desert locusts (often, these invasions stem from the Arabian Peninsula), the Horn of Africa is one of many areas which suffer locust invasions, infestations and agricultural damage. Altogether, about fifty countries suffer desert locust invasions from time to time, that is, during plague periods.

“These countries extend from West Africa to North Africa, throughout the Arab countries in the Middle East and countries in Asia, for example, India and Pakistan. The total area of desert locust plagues’ vulnerability equates to sixteen million square kilometres. So, one has to develop a deep understanding of the millions of people whose lives may become at least dislocated and, at worst, may end up dying of starvation.

“In terms of cooperation, this exists on a rather disorganised level, and obviously a lot of effort has to be put in to convince those concerned in the locust–affected countries of the benefits of organised cooperation, for example, the exchange of crucial information regarding the movements of swarms. Part of the problem is the political aspect; there are serious tensions between some of the countries concerned – the Somalis and Ethiopians refuse to talk to one another at the diplomatic level. The southern part of Ethiopia is virtually populated by Somalis, so the Ethiopians believe that, at some point, the Somalis from outside Ethiopia will try to take over the main province in Ethiopia, occupied by Somalis; the province is called Ogaden.

“So as far as our work in Somaliland is concerned, we are a small part of a much larger problem. All we can do is play our part in controlling the desert locust invasions which cross the coast and try to destroy, to the maximum extent possible, the new generations of locust hoppers. By doing this, we are helping to protect not only the food needed by the livestock in Somaliland, but also the very large areas of agriculture, which exists in the countries of East Africa.

“Now, I have to explain a very important unique aspect of the behaviour of the desert locust. Many countries in Asia, the Middle East and Africa are afflicted by invasions of different species of ravaging locusts. Whereas the African Migratory and the Red Locust had been substantially brought under control, up to the mid twentieth century, it had proved impossible to control the desert locust.

"The reason why the desert locust could not be controlled was because this species has a separate, quite different, behavioural pattern compared with other locust species. The breeding areas of the Red and African Migratory locusts are predictable; in fact, they have been mapped. These areas are usually called Outbreak Areas. So as long as those breeding areas can be patrolled, then once breeding takes place, the nymphs can be wiped out.

"With the desert locust, however, this is not the case. Over a huge geographical area of fifty countries, breeding can take place literally anywhere and at any time; with the desert locust, there are no Outbreak Areas, as such. Given the right environmental conditions, especially those relating to temperature and humidity, it will breed – period! Simply put, the behaviour of the desert locust is unpredictable, while with the other locusts, the opposite is the case. And it was this crucial difference that has made the problem of controlling the desert locust impossible to solve.

"Before I stop for today, Colin, I would mention that here in Somaliland, provided there are rains (rather than drought), we need to cope with two invasions of desert locust swarms each year. And each of these desert locust invasions, as an order of magnitude, measures about one thousand square miles. Needless to add, at peak junctures it is difficult for us in DLC to avoid a feeling of helpless frustration; we simply do not have at this time the resources to properly defend this area from locust breeding, and consequent ravenous damage by the swarms to grasslands and agriculture."

Gerald then showed me some sketches of the desert locust,

together with a small map of Somaliland, on which had been coloured in the main areas usually affected by desert locust breeding. Then, Gerald sat back in his chair a little bit and smiled at me. "So now, Colin, you know the story. What I have told you are the main points that one needs to know about the desert locusts. And if you have made your notes properly and you can understand and digest the information. I have given you, then when someone asks you, 'What is a desert locust?' you can confidently say – 'yes, I know what a desert locust is.' Have you made notes on everything I have explained to you, and do you feel confident that you now already know quite a lot about the desert locust? And do you have any questions on what I have told you?"

"Thank you, Gerald," I replied. "I am incredibly impressed at all this information you have given me; it is all completely new to me. This evening, I will write up properly all the notes which I have made. Thank you again."

For the next few weeks, I worked closely and hard with Gerald; I witnessed many aspects of the life and death of the desert locust, such as invading swarms, their ravenous destruction of vegetation, the locusts' breeding on a very large scale, finding and measuring the extent of eggfields, and so forth.

Near the end of my assignment, I learned that the director of DLC was in the country, on a field inspection trip. With the good advice of my colonel in mind, I consulted Gerald, requesting that, if possible, I wished to meet the director, Philip Stephenson. To make this happen, my jovial colleague drove two hundred miles, mainly on sandy tracks in a desolate landscape. I had the good fortune to meet and talk not only with Stephenson, but also a great man who was accompanying him – yes, the greatest of them all, Boris Uvarov, later Sir Boris, knighted by Her Majesty

Queen Elizabeth II – Knight Commander of the Order of St. Michael and St. George – K.C.M.G.

I also met a good number of desert locust field officers.

And what was my reaction, as a young nineteen–year–old, to my new experiences? In a nutshell, I felt overawed, humbled and privileged.

In due course, after my military demobilisation, I worked for two years in textiles in London. But I could not erase the memories of Africa, which almost daily flooded my imagination. So, I wrote to Philip Stephenson. He arranged for my immediate recruitment as a DLC field officer. Shortly before my twenty-second birthday, I found myself again at the DLC main base, situated in an inhospitable stony desert seven miles from the town of Hargeisa.

On arrival, I was welcomed by the senior desert locust field officer. He was responsible for desert locust control operations throughout the country; he would have been supervising and coordinating the work of about ten field officers, each of whom would be employing a labour force of, typically, some three hundred (I would succeed him later, at the age of 24). 'Oh! Colin', he said, 'Welcome to another world – *The World Of The Desert Locust.*

In 2018 my *Desert Locust Plagues* was published; the soft cover edition has been taken over by Bloomsbury Publishing (of *Harry Potter* fame).

Of the many reviews which have been written on my last book, for me, the most valuable was written by Keith Cressman of the Food and Agriculture Organization (FAO), in Rome. Cressman is regarded by most as number one in the world when it comes to control measures to be put in place to control desert locust swarms and infestations.

Included in his exhaustive review, are the following words:

The knowledge gained from his efforts with Desert Locust Control has undoubtedly contributed to … the control of the Desert Locust, that has saved an uncountable number of lives.

… (One reads about) the efforts of those incredibly committed individuals and their efforts to prevent locust swarms from forming and wreaking destruction.

… It is a modest testimony to those silent and mostly unknown efforts by so many people who continue to protect our food security.

Colin Everard's book … adds to the rich archive of the desert locust.

Dear Reader, I hope you enjoyed your visit to another world.

TWO

CONTROLLING THE DESERT LOCUST – ADVENTURES ALONG THE WAY

In what I loosely term 'the locust life', one needed to be alert and ready to sensibly respond to new situations which could suddenly develop at any tine, usually by day, although sometimes at night.

And as a side–effect to our daily work, seven days a week, one almost routinely needed to accept the reality that, without warring, one would be faced with a happening or adventure which would indeed be challenging.

I will relate two situations which are in the nature of what I have explained in the above paragraph; for each, I have included a subtitle.

SORRY!

After my appointment, at the age of 21, as a desert locust control field officer, my first assignment was to control desert locust infestations in the area north–west of the main Somali main town of Hargeisa. With the strong anti–locust campaign I had put in place, and with the work in full swing, it was during one of my inspection 'rounds' that I suffered an experience, the memory of which indelibly remains with me. Apart from the area in the vicinity of Borama (the administrative centre of the area), together with the land to the east, it was important not to neglect surveillance of the land to the west. I had already sketched possible routes which could be traversed by motor transport, including several *tougs (*wadis – riverbeds) which, provided they were not in flood, could be used.

Having given much attention to the locust infestation which needed to be controlled to the north–east of Borama, I left one day to drive to a village called Gocti, which is close to the Ethiopian border. I was accompanied by the supervisor who had been my right-hand man since my arrival in Borama. I also took with me the Issa helper. As was our routine, we took a jerry can of water, some rations, a jerry can of petrol, as well as my rifle. My 0.22 rifle would be used if we saw some guinea fowl or yellowneck (which is a francolin).

The journey initially went well. Once in Gocti, I met the local officials, after which we sat in the shade of a wall of the village police station. We had been joined by a locust scout who seemed alert and enthusiastic about his work; at that time, there were no reports of locusts in the area.

While we were eating a sandwich, we heard sudden cracks of rifle shots. Fragments of mortar from the wall above us fell on and around us. At that point, a police sergeant approached us. "Sorry for the inconvenience. We use the wall for target practice," he said. "Yes," he went on, "we have to be good shots. There are a lot of bandits around here. Once they rob someone, they just run over the border. We can't keep up with them. They are always dodging backwards and forwards. Anyway, enjoy your lunch. We will continue shooting. Nothing to worry about; the target is at least four feet above your heads. Hope there won't be a stray shot." The sergeant laughed. Then came the next burst of rifle fire and we were showered with mortar from the broken wall just above our heads. There was a pause. We quickly slipped away and left in the Land Rover.

After our abbreviated break and feeling relieved we had not stopped a stray bullet, we headed south for a few miles, where my sketch showed us we should meet the *toug*. Soon we had descended into the wide, dry riverbed. My sketch indicated that after about 20 miles of driving eastwards, we should meet the main road; this would lead us back to our camp near Borama. The first ten miles of the journey went well. The sand was quite firm, and we had little difficulty in the wide toug negotiating the remains of dead trees and boughs which littered the floor of the *toug*.

Now we were passing signs of habitation. We could see a number of women drawing water from several wells. I asked the driver to skirt the wells and give them a good berth. We seemed to progress well. Suddenly there was a lurch; the vehicle sank a little at the back – and stopped. One of the rear wheels had sunk into what seemed to be a small, probably disused, well.

We soon found some flat wood, and this was placed under a jack. The driver then began the job of jacking up the rear of the Land Rover. While this was in process, the rest of us started gathering small pieces of dead wood; these would be placed under the rear wheels to facilitate the extraction of the wheel from the well.

Then we heard a voice, "Who are you? What are you doing here?" We stood up and turned towards the voice. We were looking at a tall Issa tribesman who was standing near some bushes at the side of the toug. He was not smiling, and his intense gaze was a little unnerving. The supervisor explained who we were and what we were doing. Then this strong man said, "You have no right to be here. You are trespassers. The *toug* is reserved for our use. You should be on a road with that vehicle. You must be dealt with. I will be back with my brothers!" The man disappeared into trees and bushes. We continued our recovery work.

After about fifteen minutes, the man reappeared. Now he had his brothers with him. All carried spears. The group started chanting; now they were dancing. The chanting was growing louder. The supervisor told me they were chanting in unison, "We must kill the Outsider! We must kill the Outsider!" Feeling that the situation could become more serious and sensing that the group of Issa seemed to be working themselves into a frenzy, I decided to try and defuse a situation which was becoming more unpleasant by the second.

I advanced steadily straight at the tall leader of the group. I was relaxed and smiling. As I neared him, I motioned that I would like to inspect his spear. As my hand approached the spear, the tall Issa took one step back and at the same moment raised his spear at shoulder level. His eyes were fixed on my body. Now the tip of the spear was flashing in the sunlight, and the head of the spear was rotating quickly in short bursts. My eyes were dazzled. I felt my legs sagging and my knees were banging against one another. The limit of my vision took in only the Issa with his flashing spear. A deadly silence pervaded the scene. Abruptly, the spear rotation stopped. The tribesman drew the spear back a little and gripped the shaft more tightly. Helplessly defenceless, I waited for the inevitable. There was no escape.

At that moment, a voice pierced the tense silence. It was the steady, but stern, voice of the supervisor. Afterwards, he told me what he had said. "If you touch that man, I will shoot you between the eyes. You will be dead!" With a look of dismay, the tribesman slowly lowered the spear. Now the Issa was glaring at me. I did not move. Then, when the spear was resting at the side of the Issa, I took a tentative step backwards. I did not want to turn my back on the group. After several paces backwards, I half turned. My eyes caught the eyes of the supervisor. He held my .22 rifle in his hands; he was calm and unsmiling. He beckoned me back to the Land Rover. He told me quietly that ,as the situation became worse, he had crept inside the Land Rover and had taken out my rifle. Then he had positioned himself at one of the vehicle's doors, from which point he could take aim at the tribesman.

Soon, the vehicle had been jacked up and the dry wood and bark were in position. The driver started the engine; and again, we were *en route.* On our return at dusk to Borama, I gave a district officer a verbal report on the incident with the tall Issa tribesman.

At about seven o'clock on the following morning, a police car stopped at our camp. A sergeant and two constables told us that they should be taken immediately to the place of the previous day's incident. Ten minutes later, we were heading for the *toug*. We reached the wells and stopped.

Within a few minutes, the tall Issa was shouting at us from the edge of the *toug*. One of the policemen approached the Issa. The Issa was asked whether he still wanted to kill the Outsider. Yes, he would kill the Outsider without hesitation. The Issa was then arrested, handcuffed and brought to the Land Rover.

A day later, I found myself standing in front of a magistrate making my statement on what exactly had happened. After my statement had been read back to me, I was told to leave the courtroom. Through a doorway, I could see the supervisor and driver, who would shortly be called as witnesses.

As I left the courtroom, I found myself looking at the tall Issa; this time, he was flanked by two constables of the Somali police force. Compared with his aggressive attitude of 48 hours previously, he seemed docile and sad. As I looked into his face, he showed no emotional reaction. A few days later, the Issa helper mentioned that the tall Issa had been charged on three counts, including attempted murder. He had been sentenced to hard labour – for a period of three months!

With the digression behind us, we could devote all of our time to mounting the locust campaign. The work went well and most of the infestation was well controlled. After about six weeks of exhausting work, the escape of the surviving young locusts took place. The escaping locusts could barely form even a thin swarm. Most of the thin swarm would peter out in the following few days. Some locusts would die from weather conditions; most of the remainder would provide food for birds.

So, our locust campaign had been a success. We had played our part in destroying the locust generation which, if the control measures had not been implemented, would have flown further south with the wind in dense swarms, leaving a path of devastation as far as crops and grazing were concerned. It was not an exaggeration to state that not only hunger, but possible starvation had been avoided by the locust control measures.

A few days later, I was told that I should prepare for a move to another area which was heavily infested with locust hoppers; the area was about three hundred miles south–east of Hargeisa, the main town of Somaliland. Locally employed staff in the Borama area should be paid off, after which the supervisor and myself, with our driver, should travel to Hargeisa; I was expected there within the week. After receiving a briefing at the locust control headquarters, I would be prepared for my next locust control assignment.

Before leaving for Hargeisa about five days later, I made a few farewell courtesy calls. One of these was to the district commissioner's office. After a short chat and farewell handshake, I left the office complex by a side door. As I stepped into the sunlight, I heard a shout. Then I saw a tall, muscular man take a few steps towards me; then he seemed to jerk and stop. It was the tall Issa. I approached him; he smiled and shook my hand. Then I noticed a metal bracket around his ankle, to which was attached a chain.

I sat with the Issa tribesman for several minutes. The smile on his face faded; now he looked thoughtful and a little sad. Then he spoke through an interpreter, "I am sorry. I am very sorry. I didn't mean to kill you. We got carried away. If you need a watchman, I will look after you and your belongings. No one will dare to come near me. You don't need to pay me. But if each day, I could have a ration of rice and dates, I will be happy."

I explained to the tribesman that I would be leaving the following day. I hoped that, after serving his sentence, he would return to his clan and live peacefully. A glimmer of a smile crossed his face. Then he said, "May Allah bless you. Praise be to Allah. Nabad Gilyo – Goodbye."

GOD SAVE THE KING

At the age of 27, having gained good, hard experience in controlling plagues of the desert locust in the countries of the Horn of Africa, I was appointed to head the team whose function it was to protect the agriculture of the three countries of East Africa, namely, Kenya, Uganda and the then Tanganyika (now Tanzania).

During the first few months of my appointed time in my new function, the locust plague situation was relatively quiet. On the other hand, in southern Ethiopia, the situation was dramatically different. Over an area of some 800 square miles (about 2,000 square kilometres), dense and heavy breeding by locusts had been reported. And if this breeding infestation was not adequately controlled, then the ensuing 'escape' of the next generation of locust swarms would seriously threaten East Africa's agriculture on a very large scale.

It was therefore proposed that I should reinforce the efforts of the field officer in Southern Ethiopia. Another field officer would be diverted from his work in Somalia and would join us, near a town called El Carre.

We left with two Land Rovers and, travelling in a northerly direction from Mandera in north–eastern Kenya, the road became stony and rocky. Although we endeavoured to cover as many miles as possible during the daylight hours, in fact, in southern Ethiopia, we never exceeded an average of ten miles per hour. At Dolo, it was necessary to cross the Daua river and we found that a ferry had been constructed using oil drums with a platform above them. The river was in flood, and we had problems in positioning the Land Rover on the ferry. With considerable difficulty, the crossing was completed; a separate crossing needed to be navigated for each of the vehicles.

On reaching the field officer's camp near El Carre two days later, the reports of the widespread breeding were assessed, and we developed a plan of operation to control the infestation. The work began the following day and continued for a week. Progress was somewhat hindered due to the hostile attitude of the local inhabitants, who, from time to time, would throw themselves on to our vehicles.

Sometimes, up to ten protesting tribesmen would clamber on to a Dodge Power Wagon and try to dislocate the work. Fortunately, although many of them were armed, the tribesmen stopped short of physical aggression.

As we worked our way northwards, it became clear that the infestation extended to the north of the Webi Sciabelli river. We wished to pursue the work, but in order to achieve this, we would need to ferry insecticide and sacks of locust bait across a small river. With the help of some of the labourers, a ferry was constructed of drums, to which we lashed a platform. The next step was to carry a rope across the river, which would be attached to the ferry and used to pull it to and fro. We were warned not to enter the river since it was heavily infested with crocodiles. At this point, the supervisor of the labourers told us that he would send for 'the crocodile man'. The man appeared shortly afterwards, and it was explained that he would cast a spell over the crocodiles; the reptiles would never harm him.

Shortly afterwards, the man entered the water with a coil of rope and soon began swimming across the river, dragging the rope with him. After he had reached the other side, the rope was duly attached to the ferry of drums, and the insecticide and bait were transported across the river, followed by gangs of labourers and ourselves.

During the following few days, the work continued, and the infestation was significantly controlled.

On our return to the El Carre camp, I told my colleagues that, since the visa for entry into Ethiopia which I carried would expire within three days, I would either need to obtain an extension or, if this failed, I would have to return to Kenya.

We had heard that an Ethiopian district commissioner (DC) was based in the area, and we therefore visited his office for assistance. It was explained that he was away on a short excursion to shoot some birds; as he was expected back soon, perhaps we would like to wait in an anteroom. A bottle of anis was brought, and we were invited to enjoy a refreshing drink.

About two hours later, the Ethiopian DC appeared. He stopped outside the office in a jeep–like vehicle; he was accompanied by two fine–looking women and in the back of the vehicle were several guinea fowl which he had shot. Shortly afterwards, I was courteously received in the office of the DC. I explained the purpose of our mission to Southern Ethiopia, what we had been doing and the results which had so far been achieved. I explained the visa problem and wondered whether my visa could be extended by one week.

The DC was dressed in a khaki drill tunic, shorts and knee–high stockings; he had placed his large pith helmet on a hook inside his door. He smiled in a charming way; of course the visa could be extended. I responded that I was most grateful for his consideration, especially as I was well aware of the time–consuming formalities which normally accompanied the renewal of an Ethiopian visa.

The DC then became serious for a moment; he explained that, while he would be pleased to arrange an extension, I should understand that my passport would need to be sent to Addis Ababa. The extension process should be completed within a week or two.

"But, sir," I responded. "As I have explained, my visa expires within three days. While my passport is in Addis Ababa, my current visa will expire. What should I do then?"

"Mr. Everard, there is really no problem. I have a prison cell exactly below my office. While you are waiting for your passport to be returned, we can keep you in the cell."

I looked at the charming DC and realised that, unfortunately, we could not claim to have a meeting of minds. I politely announced that, given the circumstances, unless there was a more appropriate alternative, I would have to leave the area within the next day or so. The DC acknowledged my position.

With a twinkle in his eye, he then announced that he would be having a party later in the evening. I and my two colleagues were invited to attend. There would be plenty to drink, the guinea fowl would be cooked, and we would enjoy 'wat' and 'zigany'.

Later that evening, we were welcomed to a party of fifteen or so Ethiopians; much drink was consumed within a short period. We were then invited to eat. The 'zigany' was not simply excessively spiced, the food was laced with peppers and various other 'hot' ingredients. Within five minutes, my mouth felt as though it was on fire, and I could no longer feel my lips.

The party continued apace and by 10p.m., most of the guests were strongly intoxicated. Jokes were constantly being told (in Amharic) and each was greeted with a louder round of laughter than its predecessor.

When the party was at its height, the DC approached me. He told me that he was not only in administrative charge of this area, but he also had control of a military battalion; he was a man of power! He asked me to accompany him to a military display and, as though in haste, drove me with great confidence in the darkness along a narrow, bumpy track; eventually, we reached what appeared to be a mountainous ridge. He then asked me to observe a display of force. Immediately, much firing broke out from a group of soldiers. Many of the bullets fired were tracers; together with these, what seemed to be a type of rocket illuminated the rocky hills around us. The display lasted for about a half hour, after which the DC suggested that we should return to the party. He again drove as though in extreme haste.

By now, the party was becoming somewhat rowdy; just as I was beginning to feel that we should make a courteous exit, the DC approached me, stood in front of me and placed his hands on my shoulders. He announced that he felt that we were doing excellent work and that it would be a great pity if we could not complete our task. I agreed. Suddenly, the DC smiled at me and said, "Do you dance?"

Although taken aback, I responded that I much enjoyed dancing.

The DC then said to me, "If I play some beautiful music, will you please dance with me?"

Although the man appeared happy and harmless, and we were in public, I hesitated; I was aware that we had been invited to a party by a group of Ethiopians whose culture was different in many ways to our own. Nevertheless, why should I dance with this man? But then I would – on one condition. I thanked the DC for the invitation and said, "That is a very nice idea; although, in Europe, men do not usually dance together. If you would like to dance with me, would you consider meeting one condition? I need my visa to be extended by seven days. If you can arrange tomorrow morning for the extension to be stamped in my passport on the spot, I will dance with you."

The DC was delighted. He asked me to appear at his office the following morning at 9a.m. In the meantime, we would dance to beautiful music.

The DC asked me to wait briefly until he set his gramophone in motion. He strode across the room and leant over an ancient machine; it played only 78 r.p.m. records and it had a medium-sized 'trumpet' through which the sound would be amplified.

After winding up the machine, in the poor light he peered at the label to verify the title of the old, scratched record he wished to play. He placed the record on the turntable. The arm was then lifted and, as he lowered the needle toward the edge of the record, he glanced in my direction with a triumphant smile. The sound blared out through the scratched surface:

God save our Gracious King.
God save our Noble King.
God save the King!

The DC ran towards me and with a serene smile, said, "Shall we dance, Mr. Everard?"

We danced. I was not sure what type of step should be used for the national anthem, but experimented with hops, steps, but no jumps. The completion of the dance was greeted with loud applause.

The following morning, true to his word, the DC issued the extension. With renewed vigour, we resumed our work; we had decided to see it through to completion as quickly as possible.

Although the labourers were co–operative, we again met a hostile attitude on the part of some of the local tribesmen; they sometimes threw themselves at the trucks and clambered aboard. On one of these occasions, a truck driver became alarmed. Many tribesmen had climbed onto his vehicle; they shouted and gesticulated wildly, apparently in an endeavour to dislocate our control operations.

I became anxious when I saw our Somali driver reversing his truck towards a large *acacia* tree; it seemed he had decided to try and discourage the wild tribesmen. Within a few seconds, the tribesmen began screeching as the thorns of the tree pierced their skins; some tried to avoid the thorns by grabbing branches. The driver then accelerated away, leaving at least half of his rowdy human cargo in the tree. I pleaded with the driver not to repeat the manoeuvre; if the tribesmen became angry, their hostility could translate into physical assault. He was unmoved, and angry. He wanted to teach his fellow Somalis a lesson! Fortunately, the first lesson proved to be uniquely sufficient.

After four days, it was agreed that my colleagues and I should leave the area. I left the following morning with the two Land Rovers for the return journey to Nairobi. I estimated that it would take two days or so to reach the border with Kenya, after which, another two and a half days' drive should bring us back to Nairobi. At the time of leaving the area, there were a number of storms and we saw a great deal of sheet lightning, at night which dramatically illuminated the mountains.

A day or so later, as we slowly progressed towards Dolo, we came to a *toug* (wadi) which was in flood. One of our party waded into the flooded riverbed and, based on his report, we decided to wait an hour or so before attempting a crossing; the width of the rushing water was some twenty yards. The technique used when crossing a *toug* which was in flood was to attach a cable or rope between the two vehicles. If the first vehicle to enter the water encountered difficulties, then the rear vehicle, on land, would drag the first vehicle backwards out of the water. Once the leading vehicle had traversed the strongest part of the torrent, then it would help to pull the second vehicle to dry land on the other side. Each vehicle would enter the water as though to drive upstream; as one crossed the *toug*, one would try to steer into the direction of the rushing water. If one found that the vehicle was being pushed downstream by the force of the water, then one had two options: with the help of the second vehicle dragging one backwards, either the Land Rover would be reversed or one could accelerate and try to reach the other side before the vehicle was pushed down the riverbed.

On this occasion, we could see that there was a concrete crossing; the water was flowing over a wall which was some eight feet high. With a towrope attached to the vehicle behind me, I entered the water slowly, giving the wall as much berth as possible. Initially, with the steering turned into the torrent, progress was steady; however, at about the midpoint of the crossing, I felt the vehicle being pushed towards the edge of the wall. On this particular occasion, I took the decision to accelerate and hoped that the vehicle would pass through the point of the strongest torrent and continue to the other side of the *toug*. As I accelerated, I felt the vehicle move significantly towards the down–river edge of the wall. I immediately concluded that, unless the other vehicle could quickly reverse and drag my vehicle backwards, it was inevitable that the vehicle would be pushed over the wall by the force of the water.

Since I felt no pull backwards, I decided to abandon the vehicle. I intended to leave by the door on the side of the rushing water; I would climb on to the canopy and as the vehicle was washed over the wall I would jump away from the vehicle, separating myself as much as possible from it. In this way I hoped that, while being carried down the riverbed, I would be able to make my way to the edge of the rushing torrent.

I realised that my plan would need to be executed within a matter of seconds. Moving to the passenger side of the vehicle, I tried to open the door. To my dismay, I found that, due to the force of the torrent which thudded against the side of the vehicle and was now beginning to spill through the perspex window, it was physically beyond my strength to open the door.

Recognising that I was trapped, I waited for the vehicle to be pushed over the wall. Whether I would then be able to escape remained to be seen. The vehicle moved inexorably towards the edge of the crossing. At any second, the Land Rover would be washed over the wall and down the river on the torrent.

Then the vehicle stopped moving. Although I was in a state of anxiety, I was perplexed. I suddenly realised that the tremendous rush of water was slightly diminishing; shortly afterwards, the force of the water had been reduced to the point where I could open the door, which I did. I clambered up to the canopy and then lowered my legs over the windscreen to the bonnet.

I could see the other members of the team waving at me and shouting, but I could not hear their voices above the noise of the rushing water. After a few minutes, a driver waded into the water and shouted to me that I should stay where I was. The rope which had been attached between our vehicles had broken. Shortly afterwards, a cable was fixed to the back of the Land Rover and the rear vehicle pulled the Land Rover which I had been driving back to the water's edge.

We waited for about an hour and watched the torrent recede; we then crossed the riverbed. We stopped and walked back in the shallow water across the concrete crossing. We wondered whether a thoughtful road engineer had constructed a ridge, or perhaps a low wall, on the edge of the crossing so as to help prevent vehicles being washed downstream. We were looking for an explanation concerning why my vehicle had stopped, literally on the brink. There was no ridge.

The slow return journey continued and at last we reached Dolo.

We searched for the ferry of floating drums, but without success. After some time, we were told that the day after we had used the ferry on the outward journey, the ferry had been washed away in a flood. A new ferry was under construction, which would be ready the following day. The next afternoon, we crossed the river successfully; we continued our journey southwards to Mandera in Kenya and eventually through Wajir and Isiolo to Nairobi.

During the return journey, I had given some thought to the progress made in the technical methodology of controlling locusts. I had concluded that, although anti–locust control measures on the ground were still important, aerial reconnaissance and spraying would progressively become more significant. In consultation with Philip Stephenson, I therefore decided to take a flying licence. Like hundreds of thousands of others, I found the written and practical exercises, and tests, to be interesting; the systematic study of the theory of flight, in so many aspects, was indeed an illuminating experience.

Practical instruction was delivered between 7–8 a.m., while theory was taught in the evenings; in this way, conflict with office hours was avoided. When I had reached the 'circuits and bumps' stage, on one occasion I made a hard landing. Conforming to instructions, I taxied the aircraft to the maintenance hangar and consulted with the engineer on duty. He told me that he had noticed the hard landing. I asked him whether he wanted to check over the aircraft? He smiled,

"Open your mouth, Colin. Do you feel all right? How about your teeth?"

"I feel fine. My teeth are still there!"

"I don't think I need to check the aircraft. But I wanted to make sure that *you* have not been shaken up too much. Go back and try to make more circuits; and when we say 'bumps', we don't mean bump. Try greasing the aircraft on the runway. Once you've done it, it's a very nice feeling and you will probably be more comfortable that way."

As I progressed to the licence level, we made several testing cross–country flights. East Africa was ideal for such exercises. As one looked below, one might see vast areas of bush, semi–desert or, in the highlands, numerous valleys separated by mountain ridges; the problem was the appearance of sameness. The instructor Sven would say, "Where are we?" This was what the Americans would have described as a very good question. It was on one of those occasions that Sven taught me the importance of concentrating on the required heading, instead of becoming distracted by lengthy navigational computations; it was remarkable how one could deviate from the correct heading, while one compared the scene of confusing sameness below with the computed position on the map. By the time you had reached a conclusion (which was often wrong), the aircraft had been permitted to wander significantly from the correct heading.

Many flyers would agree that the most memorable part of their flying experience was the first solo. In my case, before taking off for that first solo circuit, the instructor crouched on the wing and repeated procedures which he had forced me to learn by heart during training. The man was a typical Scandinavian perfectionist and from the mournful expression on his face, he was evidently far more worried about the possible consequences of my flying solo than I was. I listened patiently to his monologue of repetitive instructions as though one were sitting in a church, listening to the lesson which one had heard over the years again and again. Eventually, I felt sorry for him; I patted his shoulder and tried to reassure him that I really could not see a problem in what I was about to undertake. Even if ‘icing’ should happen, he had time and again taught me how to overcome it; in the worst case, I could even make an emergency landing. I thoroughly enjoyed my first solo. It was not exciting; it was simply that one felt sufficiently confident to take the aircraft off the ground, to handle it in the air and to land it again. In fact, ‘icing’ did occur, and I felt confident in clearing the problem. On the final approach, another aircraft suddenly appeared in front of me; the student pilot had not completed the circuit properly and had cut across a corner of the circuit. A very warning light was shot from the control tower and the air traffic controller asked me to “go round again”. He then strongly rebuked the student pilot and instructed him to land forthwith.

I made my second solo circuit; again, I experienced ‘icing’ and cleared it. I made a perfect landing. The Scandinavian instructor seemed enormously relieved. This was probably because, as an experienced flyer, he knew that, in fact, things can go awry, especially during a first solo.

Although I had tried not to show my concern for the anxiety of the instructor, nevertheless I believe that he sensed it. With a somewhat perverted sense of humour, he took me shortly afterwards on some spinning exercises in a Tiger Moth, an aircraft which has an open cockpit. After stalling the aircraft at an altitude of several thousand feet, he applied the rudder in an almost vicious way. The aircraft responded correspondingly, and I was thrown against the safety straps as the aircraft spun earthwards. The noise of the rushing wind around the ears was punctuated every few seconds by the voice of Sven,

“Do something, Colin – you don’t have long to go!”

He was a hard man with a strange sense of humour, and a good instructor.

Although the intention behind my learning to fly was limited to gaining an appreciation of possibilities in controlling locusts through aerial reconnaissance and spraying, the guardian angel could see further ahead than my blinkered approach permitted at that particular juncture. The introduction to aviation helped to serve a useful purpose several years later.

In 1960, I was asked to return to Mogadishu as the Desert Locust Control (DLC) liaison officer of East Africa to Somalia. This time, I would not be a substitute for the liaison officer, who had retired; I would remain in Mogadishu for some time, and this would give me the opportunity to make the maximum contribution in terms of encouraging the government's Locust Control department to become more effective.

One always looked forward to a new assignment; at the same time, I had mixed feelings on this occasion. Politically, the situation in Somalia was gradually becoming unstable and I wondered what impact this might have on the effectiveness of the locust control measures. In addition, as a matter of policy, the East African governments were forging links with the United Nations Agencies. I recognised that this was a healthy development; however, I had already met one or two desert locust control 'UN experts' and had not been impressed with the quality of these men. One could only hope for the best; I for one would do my utmost to achieve the best results in what would be a changing work environment.

THREE

THE TIP OF THE HORN OF AFRICA

In 1957, I was asked to support the Somali anti–locust effort, which entailed residing in Mogadishu for the duration of my assignment. As a centre of trade, Mogadishu had existed for about a thousand years. After visits by Greek vessels in ancient times, its development had been greatly influenced by Arab countries to the north. In fact, over the centuries, the Somali coastal area, including Mogadishu, was ruled by a series of Sultans.

In the 19th century, the Italians arrived as colonizers. As a part of Italian East Africa, heavy investment was made in the transportation system, as well as in agriculture. The flagship tarmac road project was the *Strada Imperiale*; this was a road planned and constructed, mainly using Italian labour, to link Mogadishu with Addis Ababa in Ethiopia. When completed, the road would cover a distance of some one thousand kilometres. As far as agricultural development was concerned, much investment was made in banana production, especially along the banks of the two large rivers which flow through the southern part of Somalia; these rivers are called the Webi Schiabelli, which means Leopard River, and the Juba.

At the time of my arrival in Mogadishu, it was a small city that functioned well. Apart from Arab–type buildings, there were a number of older buildings which, typically, were supported by imposing, heavily built, weathered walls. Especially in the centre of the city, there were a good number of white buildings which had been erected during the era of Italian colonization. So, the appearance of the centre of the city was a mixture of buildings that reflected the cultures of Arab countries and Italy. The mixture of styles was rather pleasing to the eye. Inland, behind the city, the ground rose towards a long ridge. Standing on the ridge, one could admire the white and darker coloured buildings which bordered the vastness of the Indian Ocean, normally a calm sea that seemed to stretch forever to the horizon.

Regarding the efforts to establish a database to improve ant locust measures in all affected countries, significant progress had been made. For instance, research into ground–level spraying techniques resulted in vehicles being equipped with a drum of insecticide, from which a spray was pumped using the force of the vehicle's exhaust. Developing spraying techniques, whether on the ground or in the air, posed the challenge of controlling the size, dosage and concentration of the spray droplets. The primary goal was to ensure that the droplet size would never lead to excessive spray concentrations, as these could endanger animal and plant life. Conversely, if the spray droplet size was too small, the spray would diffuse into the atmosphere, with the droplets sometimes moving upwards instead of downwards towards the locusts. By 1957, it was evident that the use of vehicles fitted with insecticide spraying gear would replace the manual labour in many locust–infested areas.

Subsequently, I found myself considering the overall locust situation in north–eastern Somalia at that time, and I questioned whether our knowledge of locust movements and behaviour was sufficient, or if there were unanswered questions.

This led me to identify what I thought might be an important question regarding locust migratory routes. Detailed knowledge of migratory routes was crucial for positioning our field personnel correctly in the right areas and in good time to prepare and carry out locust control campaigns.

As far as locust invasions of the northern part of the Somali Peninsula were concerned, typically, locust swarms arrived from the north and northwest during August and September, covering an area of about one thousand square miles. Although little was known about where the locusts rested before flying south from mid–October onwards, there was an assumption that the locusts held up in the hills and mountains which straddle from east to west the northern Somali area. It was assumed that the swarms remained in the mountains until they moved southwards to breed; one sometimes heard a reference that swarms were harboured in the Erigavo hills in the northeast of Somaliland.

However, because we received few reports of locust swarms in the mountainous area during the late summer months, I questioned this assumption. Could it be, for example, that the swarms moved further east towards the tip of the Horn of Africa? If they could be found, then they could be controlled in situ. This action would greatly diminish the escaping swarms which would fly to the south to breed, once the northeast monsoon would establish itself several weeks later.

With this in mind, I asked for a meeting with senior members of the Somalia Locust Control Organization. After explaining what I thought we needed to know, I asked whether the Somalis had made a locust information–gathering reconnaissance in the far north of the country. My question was met with silence. The blank expressions on the faces of my colleagues gave me the answer. Then the senior of the group, Ali Nur, spoke.

"Colin, no, we haven't been up there, and we don't know much about the area. We certainly have no idea whether locust swarms invade the area. You have to understand that we are mostly from tribes who live in the lower half of the country. So, I don't think we would be welcomed up there; after all, we are talking about an area which is at least fifteen hundred kilometres to the north of here. If we were to travel up there, who knows, we could be killed!"

"Thank you," I responded, "I think this is an important subject. After all, if we find out that swarms congregate somewhere near Cape Guardafui, which is the tip of the Horn of Africa, then we could carry out control measures and perhaps hit the generation of adults so hard that control of the next generation further south would be much easier. I will plan to make a trip up there from mid May. Fortunately, as a European, I don't have to think about other tribes."

Preparations for my trip were routine. I was used to reconnaissance work throughout most of the Horn of Africa. In this case, there was an intriguing difference with the norm, in the sense that I would be travelling to a remote area which, up to that point, had not been reconnoitred by locust control personnel.

The day before leaving with two Land Rovers for the first stage of the journey, I was working on last-minute tasks in my office. There was a tap on the door. It was Ali Nur. He said simply, "Colin, I understand you are leaving tomorrow. You know, you may be in for a few surprises up there in the north, who knows – only Allah! We don't like the idea of you going up there with just a driver and helper. I would like to come with you."

The next day, we left for a town called Belet Uen; the town was close to banana plantations, and it straddled a river called *Webi Sciabelli* (river of leopards). Along the way, Ali Nur contacted locust scouts; their main task was to keep their area under surveillance and report on locust movements. However, there were no assistants in the extreme north of the country. Apparently, for an unexplained reason, the Somali Locust Control Organization excluded the extreme north from their sphere of work.

The road to Belet Uen was of tarmac, having been constructed by the Italian colonizers; they used mainly Italian labourers for the construction. The journey was pleasant as it followed the course of the Webi Schiabelli river. We camped about an hour's drive beyond Belet Uen. Now, instead of driving further west, we took a road which would lead to Galcaio, to the north.

In this part of the world, one normally hoped to cover about 200 miles (320 kilometres) each day; this would be a good average. Faster vehicular travel on dirt roads was the exception; sometimes, roads had become pot holed to such an extent that a top speed of 10 m.p.h. could hardly be reached. Rain damage could also present a problem. In the Horn area, there are usually two annual rainy periods; otherwise, the country receives no rainfall. When the rains come, intense storms may occur. So, the road traveller should never be surprised to suddenly find that stretches of a road had been virtually washed away. There were other hazards; for example, small bridges which had been damaged by the elements, which would confront the patient driver, and which would need to be overcome. This situation was accepted as part of the everyday working life of the locust officer.

Now we were en route to Galcaio, a provincial town which was situated in central Somalia. For a hundred or more miles to the south and north of Galcaio, one drives across a vast gypsum plain. The Land Rover is continuously battered with bumps and vibrations as one traverses the gypsum rock. Tons of gypsum dust belch behind the Land Rover, causing a dense cloud. Some of the dust is forced upwards, so that it is not long before the driver and passengers feel a grittiness on their tongues. From time to time, our Somali driver would spit out of the window.

Although we had intended making a camp for the night near Galcaio, I suggested we should press on further north towards Gardo. I hoped we would leave the gypsum behind, which we did. I had spent some seven months working from Las Anod, in Somaliland to the west of Galcaio. Las Anod too was a town situated on gypsum. I soon learned the local water was brackish. So, a short drink had the effect on the stomach of salts! Working from Las Anod, in order to replenish our supply of drinking water, we travelled 50 miles to the north, to Hudin. There we approached a cave in an outcrop of rocks. Having frightened away a colony of baboons, we removed a boulder and entered the cave. Crawling along a low natural tunnel, after about 25 yards we came to a deep pool of fresh water. From this fresh water source, we could replenish our galvanized water drums.

In any case, the brackish water had made an indelible mark on my memory because of its explosive effect on the stomach. With this in mind, we continued driving until twilight, and a little beyond. The gypsum terrain had gradually given way to sandy, broken country and the low bushes and small plants reflected the change in the terrain. I asked the driver to stop when he could see an acacia tree not far from the narrow dirt road. We carried on; with the short twilight which is normal in countries not far from the equator, the light seemed to be dwindling. Then I saw the driver switch on his headlights. Suddenly, he stopped. Before I could speak, the driver opened his door and crouched by the wing of the Land Rover. Now in the headlamps

I could see a gazelle; it was walking straight towards the front of the vehicle, seemingly in a daze; it was dazzled by the glare of the lights. Then I saw the driver's hand grab a leg of the animal.

'Bis–mily–raham–rahim.' Five seconds later, the animal was dead; its throat had been slit by the driver's knife.

That evening, in our little camp under a green umbrella acacia tree, the Somalis had a feast and recounted stories to one another until midnight. And I was served a dinner of filet steak by the cook and general helper, who was travelling with us.

Next morning, we awoke later than usual. At about six o'clock, as I slipped out of my bed from under the mosquito net, I saw that we had company. Five or six young bushmen were standing in a semi–circle around our camp. Each was dressed in a loin cloth and simple leather sandals; their torsos were gleaming in the tentative rays of the rising sun. Each carried a massive, dense head of crinkly hair. All looked impressively strong. Each of these fine–looking men held a spear at his side.

I pulled on my shorts and approached the group. They made no gesture. I held out my hand.

"Peace. Do we have peace?" I said in Somali. The men looked at me, without movement nor gesture.

I continued, "I am speaking to you in your own Somali language. Listen. Do we have peace?"

The look on each face became more intense. For about ten seconds, these men fixed me with a steady stare. Suddenly, one man let out a shrill cry. Now, all were singing in unison. Then they danced in a circle. Finally, each approached me, smiling, and took my hand, exclaiming, "Peace!"

Once we had explained our mission, each of our visitors became relaxed and friendly; their curiosity had been satisfied. The men related where and when they had seen locusts over the last year or two. While we were talking, two of the men ran off. They rejoined us a half hour later carrying a wooden pot, which was full of camel's milk; nowadays, the milk of a camel is recognized as being highly nutritious. After two hours of questioning and counter–questioning, we were again en route, continuing northwards to Gardo.

The vast gypsum plain was well behind us and now we were traversing mostly sandy country which, typically, would be ideal for locust breeding. Apparently, there had been rainfall because the bushes were green and, here and there, we could see ephemeral growth. Sometimes we stopped and spent an hour or so looking for locusts. In fact, we usually found a few, although they were solitary and showed no signs of swarming.

As we progressed northwards, I was struck by the contrast between the relatively pleasant semi-desert conditions through which we were driving and the changed scene which would confront the traveller in the period of the second half of June to October. It is during this period that the summer wind, the *kharif*, blows. This is a wind of incredible intensity; the wind carries huge amounts of dust and sand in its path. And for weeks at a time, those who live in villages survive in a daily gloom, itself accompanied by the noise of the howling, gale–force wind.

Once we reached Gardo, Ali Nur lost no time in contacting the Locust Assistant, who told us all he knew about locusts in the area. We then drove on and, before stopping for the night, we suddenly found ourselves near a quite large, cultivated area. The contrast with the sandy, semi–desert conditions was striking. Before our eyes were date palms, fruit trees, maize and vegetables. Soon the workers ran towards us. They explained that there had been some rainfall in the last few weeks. Now, with the hot sunshine, the crops were flourishing.

"Have you seen any locusts?" I asked.

"Not this year so far, but last year a huge swarm arrived. It stayed here for two weeks – and it ate absolutely everything! It was very sad; we had worked so hard for many months. Then everything was lost!"

This was the first confirmation of the presence of a large locust swarm in the general area, which was, in fact, not very far from the tip of the Horn of Africa. And if this swarm had flown so far east, without doubt others took a similar route; in its gregarious phase, the desert locust would always tend to join other swarms.

On the next day, we continued to press northwards. The sandy landscape gradually gave way to stony terrain, which soon became a desert of small stones and gravel. We had now entered what one might call a moonscape. The altitude was rising and by mid–afternoon we had reached a village called El Gal. There, the villagers told us that, although a road through the mountains to the coast had been planned, construction had hardly started. So, if we wished to reach the coast, we could only traverse the mountains on foot. Our belongings could be transported by camels; we could hire burden camels on the spot, which we did.

I was intrigued, that camels, an animal of the desert, could be used in the stony mountains. The camel driver explained that these were specially bred for the mountains; the breed was stockier than the camels of the desert. These animals had been trained to obey commands, usually for caution; these commands were loud and guttural. I soon learned some of the commands and the animals reacted perfectly. As these animals found their way through the maritime escarpment, I was frequently amazed how they navigated tricky, sometimes dangerous, stretches. Helped by the commands of their driver, throughout the journey they were always sure–footed.

After walking for about three hours, we decided to camp in the mountains overnight; we were now about two thousand feet above sea level. Although we were on stony ground, there was an abundance of bushes and small trees around us. Before leaving shortly before five o'clock on the following morning, I had been woken up by a heavy dew; with saturated sheets, I was encouraged to get out of bed! Now we were again on the move. After an hour or so, we reached the crest of a ridge. From there we could see the sea stretching in the early sunlight to the horizon. This was the Gulf of Aden, a southern extension of the Red Sea.

Four and a half hours later, we reached a village on the coast called Durbo. For the last part of the walk, the track descended very steeply; the camels, in particular, needed patient and careful guidance to prevent the animals from stumbling. Compared with the conditions of the previous few days, the temperature had soared to the level often found on the shores of the Red Sea; and the humidity level was uncomfortably high.

In Durbo, I soon found the resident district officer; like most Somali government officers, he was apparently new in his work. I explained the purpose of our reconnaissance and my plan to reach Cape Guardafui. The young district officer, who struck me as having great interest in what we were doing, told us all he knew about locust sightings.

But he seemed troubled with our plan to reach Cape Guardafui. He explained that, due to poor road communications, only rarely could one travel far on existing dirt tracks. For example, east of Durbo, the Italians had established a fishing school, which included a mini tunny fish canning factory. The lighthouse on Guardafui was maintained and operated by an Italian. These men were invariably delivered to their place of work by sea; they would never risk trying to use a road system which was thoroughly unreliable. He personally doubted that we could reach Cape Guardafui.

The district officer gave us geographical and agricultural information about the coastal area. Some of the so–called littoral was stony and some was suitable for date production. He emphasized that this northern area felt little connection with the government in Mogadishu. And he felt the reverse was true. So, in a sense, once one reached the northern coastal area, effectively one found oneself in a different country, a country which had different values, a different lifestyle and different priorities.

I explained that we would prepare for the walk to Alula, a distance of about 50 miles. The district officer invited us to a lunch of rice and dates. Throughout, the conversation was a delight. The district officer was not only a well–educated person; he had a happy, sometimes jovial personality. Towards the end of the meal, he said, "I have to tell you, I admire what you are doing. If one day it will be possible to control locusts, this would be a wonderful achievement. I personally have seen crops devoured; and I have seen a lot of hunger, even starvation, caused by the destruction of crops. I feel very motivated to support your efforts. So, I have been thinking how I could support you. Now I have an idea. I have the use of an old Italian four–wheel drive vehicle. It's not in good condition, but if you would like to use it as you wish, you are welcome. I can also offer the services of a driver. He certainly knows his way around here. You can return the vehicle on your return. Good luck!"

An hour later, we were en route to Alula. At times, the coastal area was quite wide; at other times, the cliffs of the maritime escarpment almost reached the sea. Apart from crossing the mouths of huge riverbeds, some with walls which were over 150 feet deep, we traversed date plantations.

In one area where rocky terrain protruded almost to the shoreline, I noticed rough, craggy, seemingly somewhat stunted trees rooted in black rocks the bulbous root in the rock was an extraordinary sight. Shortly after, we saw a man holding a large, heavy, dagger–like knife. With this instrument he was stabbing the rough bark of one of the trees which had forced its way through a rock face. Curious, we asked him what he was doing. He explained that this was a frankincense tree. By removing part of the bark, he would have access to the tree's aromatic resin; this would soon harden.

About once a week, an Arab dhow appeared near the coastline and dropped its anchor. Those who extracted frankincense could sell their collection to the Arabs. Eventually, the frankincense would find itself as a valuable ingredient of the highest quality perfumes, mainly in Europe, North America, perhaps even in Japan; or it would be burned in Christian churches throughout the world.

With this explanation, my memory took me back to a visit I had made a few years previously to Upper Egypt. I recalled a beautifully preserved wall painting in the temple of Queen Hatshepsut, which illustrated the Egyptian boatmen bringing frankincense from the Land of Punt. And now, some 3,500 years later, I was witnessing part of a similar story.

As a brief aside, after the political fragmentation, twenty–five or so years ago, of what was the Somali Republic of the sixties, the self–proclaimed autonomous state in northern Somalia is today called Puntland.

About halfway to Alula, we called on the fishing school. After a few minutes, the principal appeared; he was a short, stocky man, clad only in a pair of lightweight khaki shorts. "Be quick," he blurted out, "I'm a busy man. I can give you not more than five minutes. Be quick!"

"Thank you," I responded. "Did you ever see locusts around here?"

"Locusts? My God! Yes! About eighteen months ago, this whole area was invaded. I will never forget it. They blotted out the sun; can you believe that? It's true! We thought the swarm came from the direction of Arabia. But when they crossed the coast, there must have been some wind in the upper air, which blew some of the locusts back out to sea. The locusts may have been weak after their long flight. Anyway, thousands, perhaps millions, fell into the sea. The sea was yellow over a huge area; yes, the sea was covered with drowned yellow locusts. The sea became a huge yellow carpet. They made wonderful food for the tunny fish."

The principal looked at his watch. "That's it," he said. "I'm a busy man! Goodbye." Yes, he was indeed a busy man, who lived and worked in one of the most remote areas of our world! Our locust informant disappeared through a swing door. I was left to wonder at this dedicated man, a man who seemed to us to be working in the middle of nowhere, with his brown torso and scanty shorts. And he had little time for a passerby.

We reached Alula in the afternoon and spent the rest of the afternoon and most of the following day gathering locust information. The district commissioner was a helpful person. Like most officials, he spoke Italian, but no English. Conversing in Somali, he explained that the road beyond a village called Bereda had been completely washed away. Between Bereda and Guardafui, the high ground extended to the sea. One might consider climbing, scrambling and walking to Guardafui.

However, he strongly advised against this approach. With the high temperatures and the degree of exertion needed for perhaps a day and a half, physical exhaustion could not be ruled out. If the walker collapsed, little could be done to save the person.

In the circumstances, his advice was to drive to Bereda in the evening and ask the villagers for advice on how to travel further east. If the villagers were to tell us that we could not go further, then we could spend a day there to gather locust information. Then we should start our return journey.

In the evening, we left for Bereda, arriving in Bereda at about midnight. To our surprise, a number of villagers were awake to greet us. Although no mention had been made by the District Commissioner, it seemed that a forerunner had been sent from Alula to Bereda to let the villagers know that we would be visiting them. After words of welcome and 'Peace', the Chief of the villagers spoke.

"It is our understanding that you would like to reach Guardafui. Beyond our village, the road is no more. You cannot walk by the sea because of the cliffs which will bar your way. So here we have two canoes for you, and we can transport you on the sea to a village called Olloch. Then, after a further short journey to Darmo, you can walk to Guardafui in a few hours. If you leave here at two o'clock in the night, you should reach Olloch by about sunrise.

"I need to make one important point quite clear. You make this journey at your own risk. We use the canoes at night because the sea is usually calmer at night. But you never know. The sea can become treacherous at any time. Now, don't forget that there are many sharks in the sea. So, if the canoe capsizes, then it could be very dangerous. As I said, it is important that you understand what could happen."

En route to Cape Guardafui, the tip of the Horn of Africa

We left Bereda in two dug–out canoes at two o'clock in the morning. The sea was calm and above us shone a beautiful, clear moon. As I stepped into the canoe, I asked what I should do to help. One of the paddlers said, "You are a tall man. If you move from one side to another, the canoe may capsize. That would be the end for us because in the sea we will die. Our Chief told you that. We know what we are doing. We want you to lie along the bottom of the canoe. Please lie still! We will tell you when you can move."

I obeyed instructions. Now we were about a hundred yards offshore and moving smoothly through the calm water. I lay still, hearing the regular strokes of the paddle. I looked at the clear moon; and perhaps I closed my eyes and dozed a little. At about five o'clock, the paddler announced that we had reached Olloch. The sea was shallow where the canoe beached, so when I left the canoe, I had quite a long walk through the gentle surf.

As I reached the shoreline, it seemed that all the villagers were running towards us. Soon, we found ourselves the centre of a good number of villagers who, apparently, were curious as to why we had stopped to visit them. These were happy, laughing people, bubbling with excitement. They talked and asked questions continuously. Now one or two began to gently stroke my arms. Yes, for some, this was the first time they had seen, and could even touch, a human being having skin of white pigment. What an experience for them!

After the initial burst of excitement, I began to ask questions about locusts. Of course, the villagers had seen swarms from time to time. But, they explained, locusts were not their current priority. They were plagued not by locusts, but by packs of hyenas. If I knew how to control locusts, then surely, I could tell them how to control hyenas! Apologizing for my lack of hyena control knowledge, we returned to the canoes.

We continued our canoe journey, with the canoe being beached at a small village called Darmo. By now, the sun was well up and we could already feel its heat; from now on, it would only get hotter by the hour. The villagers directed us to walk up the hill behind their village; then we should walk in an easterly direction until the lighthouse came into view. This was Cape Guardafui, the tip of the Horn.

The next 40 minutes proved to be the most exhausting walk of my life. For this period, we toiled up an extremely steep hill in soft, fine, deep sand. It seemed as though we were ascending

The tip of the Horn of Africa. (the author stands on the right)

a huge, incredibly high, sand dune. With the heat of the sun bearing down on us, we had the challenging task of making progress in the soft sand. Sometimes, strive as we might, we could make no progress at all. Our feet simply sank into the sand and dragged us backwards. Then we would try again. We were doing our best, but would it be enough?

At last, the ground became firmer. Although we felt extremely tired, we told ourselves we were on the crest of what was a massive hill of soft sand. In fact, the ascent equated to an altitude difference of 800 feet. As we began the walk to Guardafui, I realized my feet and ankles had been burned by the hot sand. We continued walking. At the higher elevation, the heat was tempered by a breeze. After an hour or so, the lighthouse came into view.

A half hour later, we had reached Cape Guardafui, the tip of the Horn of Africa.

A Somali approached and shook our hands. He admitted to feeling surprised. Visitors were extremely rare, especially those on foot. He explained that the lighthouse keeper and other employees always arrived and departed by boat. I asked him if he had ever seen locusts in the area. He told us the previous year the entire sandy peninsular had been heavily infested with breeding locusts. So, this meant an area of roughly ten by five miles had been infested. He said that practically all the vegetation which grew on the peninsular had been devoured.

While we were talking, the lighthouse keeper joined us. Alfredo Polidari introduced himself and welcomed us. He led us into the lighthouse and climbed a metal spiral staircase. Standing on a platform, we could see the whole sandy peninsular. To our right was the Gulf of Aden, which would join the Red Sea, and on our left, the Indian Ocean stretched to the horizon.

Alfredo proudly showed us the interior of the lighthouse. Most major parts were protected by highly polished brass plating. The entire mechanism struck me as well organized, and everything looked in impeccable condition.

Alfredo had operated and maintained the lighthouse for two years. He lived in a small building nearby. Apart from a shed, there were no other buildings. Alfredo had a pretty, young Somali wife who looked after him and conversed in Italian. Apart from a few chickens and a stand of tomatoes, the landscape was barren.

Alfredo seemed to be a thoroughly self–sufficient person. He struck me as a calm man who was content with life. However, when I explained that we should soon start the return journey, he reacted with firmness.

"You mean you have come all this way to spend an hour or two with us? You don't understand! You are a rarity in this part of the world. You will stay the night. And tomorrow, I will have the pleasure of serving an Englishman his English breakfast. You will stay!"

We spent the hours till dusk collecting samples of shrubs and plants, some of which I had never seen. Although my knowledge of Italian is superficial, we talked easily to one another. Alfredo was *au courant* with current affairs; for example, he was well informed on the Suez crisis.

After some supper, we slept well. Next morning, I had hoped to depart by seven o'clock at the latest. But Alfredo had other ideas. He asked me to look around the lighthouse; he would call me as soon as breakfast was ready. After about half an hour, I heard a call; I descended to ground level and walked into a small building. Alfredo was beaming.

"Please come and sit down at the table. Here is your English breakfast."

I sat down. The table was beautifully laid with a tablecloth of embroidered cotton. Before me was a very large omelette. In fact, it was the largest omelette I had ever seen; so, on Cape Guardafui, I experienced another 'first' in my life.

"Oh! Alfredo, this is wonderful. But you know, the omelette is huge. May I please offer you half?"

Alfredo smiled. "I never eat breakfast! We made the omelette with twelve eggs. You are an Englishman. Please enjoy your breakfast."

I persevered. After a few minutes, Alfredo jumped up. He grabbed a matching embroidered serviette and handed it to me. He tapped his head – how forgetful!

While I was meeting the latest challenge, this time the huge omelette, Alfredo and I talked a little. I asked him about visitors. He told me that during the last two years he had received two visitors, who were together. One was a Catholic priest who, unfortunately, had suffered a heart attack. The priest died. Alfredo pointed to a grave about a hundred metres away where the priest had been buried. Alfredo mentioned that he had dug the grave himself.

At the end of the sumptuous meal, it was time to leave. I was wondering about the effect of the sun on an overfed human being. Soon, with goodbyes in Somali, Italian and English, we were walking away from Cape Guardafui. After scrambling down the huge, hot hill of sand, below the peninsular, we reached Darmo. Soon we were heading back by canoe along the coast to Olloch and onwards to Bereda. Again, for stability of the canoe, I lay outstretched in the bottom of the canoe; as protection against the sun, a strip of sackcloth had been thrown over me. At Bereda, we bade adieu to the villagers and reached Alula in the four–wheel drive vehicle at nightfall.

On the following day, we drove to Durbo, where we returned the vehicle to the district commissioner. He was very interested in what we had found out about locust movements and breeding in the northern area. For our part, he received from us deep appreciation that we had had the use of the vehicle.

"I hope you didn't look underneath the old vehicle," he said. "If you had, I don't think you would have risked your lives in it!" he added with a laugh.

"No," I replied. "We didn't look underneath – and we have arrived in one piece. So, thank you again."

As we said goodbye, the district officer mentioned that the wind would soon change from predominantly north–east to south-west, the so–called *kharif.* The *kharif* would blow for four months or so and, as in each year, it would harm the environment, causing huge sand drifts and blowing dust and sand over vast areas. He told us the last Arab dhow of the season had left for Aden the previous evening – a sure sign that the wind was expected to change its direction.

Now we turned our attention to what lay before us. We were faced with the formidable walk up and through the mountains. Once we had reached the top of the escarpment, we would have to walk about three and a half hours to the Land Rovers which we had left at El Gal. We thought the walk through the mountains to the crest would take about four hours.

Because of the intense heat and humidity, we decided to delay the start of our walk for about an hour and a half. We would leave Durbo at about half past two, hoping that the temperature might cool about an hour after the start of our walk. However, the camels would walk more slowly. So, they could leave with our belongings and water without waiting for us to start. Without more ado, the camels left for the walk through the mountains.

Shortly before leaving at the agreed time, a man of about thirty sat down and asked us what we were doing and where we were going. When we told him, he said, "That's good news. I am from around here. I am also leaving for the top of the mountains. If you agree, we can go together. I have walked up there a few times. I'm lucky. I know a short cut. It's steep at first, but then it gets easier. At the top, the short cut crosses the camel track. If you like, I will be your guide. Then you can wait for the camels on the ridge at the top. And if you come with me, you won't be so tired – it's quicker!" Turning to a youth, he added, "This is my nephew. He is coming too."

After talking to Ali Nur, we agreed to follow this pleasant

man. Shortly after, we left. We had nothing to carry; the helper, however, carried a goatskin of water.

Our guide was right. The first hour and a half of the walk was arduous and physically challenging. Although the temperature was steadily dropping, it was still hot, and the high humidity encouraged me to take off my shirt because my shirt and shorts were saturated with perspiration. The so–called short cut led us over rocks and stony ground. Sometimes the little–used track disappeared altogether. We pressed on – and up.

Suddenly, I heard a thump behind me. The helper had collapsed with exhaustion. As he fell, the goatskin of water slipped from his hand. We did what we could, which was not very much, to revive the helper. The goatskin of water had lost about three quarters of its contents. After a few minutes, the helper opened his eyes; he seemed disoriented, staring in different directions as though to recapture his bearings. After about ten minutes, Ali Nur and I supported the helper as he tried to stand up. We put his arms around our shoulders and walked slowly ahead; the helper was part carried and part dragged.

Now we had reached an altitude of 2,500 feet above sea level. We found ourselves on the ridge of a mountain. Nightfall would descend in about 45 minutes. When would we cross the main camel track? One hoped soon. Now the helper had recovered to the point where he could walk without assistance. So now our group, although feeling extremely tired, was reasonably mobile.

Suddenly, our guide stopped. He looked a changed man. He feverishly looked around as though he wanted to escape. His lips were trembling. I took his arm and asked him to tell us what had happened. Almost whispering, with short, seemingly breathless bursts of words, he announced that he had lost his way. Now he realized we were too far west. To reach the camel track, we would need to descend into the valley and work our way up the mountain to the east. The ridge on the next mountain would lead us to the camel track.

In our pitiful state of near–exhaustion, we simply glared at this man, a so–called guide who had brought us to the wrong place, a place where we found ourselves alone and vulnerable in an inhospitable range of mountains. Of course, we were shocked. The helper broke the silence. Looking at me, he said, “Can we kill him – now!”

Standing on that remote mountain ridge and fearful of what might happen to us, I for one could understand his outburst. In basic terms, this was a young man who felt he had been deceived and now he was becoming frightened of his possible fate. Nevertheless, no, the guide who had hopelessly misled us would not be murdered.

For our part, we found ourselves in a new, unexpected situation. First, we had separated ourselves from our water, which was somewhere being carried on a camel’s back. Second, in our fatigued state, we were faced with a strenuous task, in fading light, which involved scrambling down a mountainside and climbing the next mountain to a ridge where, we hoped, we would find the main camel track. We briefly considered sleeping where we found ourselves and carrying on at dawn. But this possibility was quickly rejected. We were without water, and we could not ignore the possibility that wild animals might find us. The uninhabited mountains were ideal habitats for animals such as lion and leopard.

So, after our short rest, we set off again and descended the mountainside. Having reached the narrow floor of the valley rather sooner than I had expected, we prepared ourselves for the final ascent of the mountain side which towered above us. With the setting sun and with the higher altitude, I began to gain a feeling of regenerated strength.

We began the walk up the scree, which was strewn over the surface of the mountain. Gradually, the scree gave way to large stones; and shortly after, we found ourselves navigating our path through boulders. Suddenly, we were faced with a rock face which was at least 50 feet high. After traversing the mountain below the rocks, we found we could climb on to a lower rock. From our pedestal, we could progress over the higher level of the rocks. Here and there the surface of the rocks was broken, so we would either jump over the cracks, or we would need to make a detour to circumvent the gullies.

At a point where we thought we had crossed the massive rocks, I slipped in a gulley. I did not fall far, but I felt shaken; so, I rested for five minutes. We then noticed that the skin had been torn from my ankle. Having tied a handkerchief around the wound, we hoped the blood would eventually congeal, which it did. We carried on, always steadily gaining altitude.

Just as dusk fell and the darkness enveloped us and our surroundings, we suddenly found ourselves crossing the main camel track. After taking a few steps, we lay down on the stony ground to rest; around us, I could see silhouettes of bushes and low trees. At an altitude of 3,000 feet above sea level, the air was cool, and the breeze wafted gently over our weary limbs. I for one felt relieved that at last we had found the camel track.

I turned to Ali Nur.

"Well, Ali, we made it, thank goodness. It's about three hours' walking to El Gal, where the Land Rovers are. I wonder where our camels are; do you think they have already passed here?"

Before Ali Nur replied, the unmistakable noise of wooden camel bells pierced the night air. Five minutes later, the camels had arrived. We had soon cut thorny acacia branches to make a small zariba fence. Then we slept.

Shortly before five on the following morning, we set off for El Gal. There we transferred to the waiting Land Rovers and drove in a southerly direction to a town called Scuscuiban. The word SCU–SCIU–BAN is an alliteration to sound like the frothing water which tumbles into a nearby water hole. Surface water north of the river Webi Schiabelli, which is in the southern part of the country, is practically unknown. Scusciuban is one of the very few exceptions.

As far as my ankle was concerned, it had become swollen, and I had almost lost the use of my foot. I enquired whether there was a medical facility in the town. I was directed to a house where I could consult Dr. Parisi, a medical doctor provided to Somalia by the World Health Organization. Dr. Parisi, a charming and interesting man, cleaned the wound, apologizing that he would unavoidably hurt me. With my foot encased in medical dressing and bandages, Dr. Parisi said, "The whole thing is a mess, I am afraid. I hope I have done enough. You won't leave my house for three days. You will stay in my bed the whole time. I will sleep on the sofa in the living room. I will decide in three days if you are fit to travel."

Three days later, with my ankle on the mend, we drove south, reaching Mogadishu after five days of driving. There, my ankle received more medical attention; in time, it healed.

Apart from the reports which needed to be compiled, as well as sketch maps which showed likely areas for locusts breeding, I sent 33 samples of bushes to the herbarium in Kenya. The accompanying list showed where and when each specimen had been found, together with its Somali name (I was fluent in the Somali language). I later received a letter to tell me that at least one of the species was new to the recorded flora of Africa.

So, what had we achieved on this reconnaissance? We had clearly found out that, contrary to assumption, locust swarms moved much further eastwards at certain times of the year in the northern part of Somalia. In fact, they sometimes bred on a very large scale as far east as Cape Guardafui.

Resulting from this fact, by obtaining accurate locust information throughout the year, using a locust scouting system, it should be feasible to mount campaigns to destroy locusts and their progeny in the extreme northern area of Somalia. By reducing the locust escape from the north, the scale of subsequent breeding in the south would be greatly reduced. Not only would agriculture and grazing be spared from destruction by ravaging swarms, the cost of mounting large–scale locust campaigns in breeding areas further south, would be much reduced.

In a nutshell, we had made yet another contribution to piecing together the complex jigsaw of the picture of locust movements and likely breeding areas in the Horn of Africa.

En passant, looking back, we can hardly believe that Somalis in the 20th century could lead peaceful lives, rarely threatened by violence. Tragically, Somalis have moved into the 21st century. Now, the northern part of Somalia is plagued by pirates, together with the violence which accompanies their criminal activities.

Four years later, in 1961, I made another reconnaissance in the northern part of Somalia. Instead of reaching Cape Guardafui from the towns of Alula and Bereda on the northern coast, I travelled up the eastern coast along the shore of the Indian Ocean. In addition to gathering information on possible breeding areas and so forth, I needed to verify small, but important, pieces of data compiled during my earlier reconnaissance in 1957. It was during the second reconnaissance that I investigated the presence of desert locusts in an area south of Alula; this was called the Hemistio Depression. To digress, at that time, the Somali language was usually in the oral form; nowadays, Hemistio would be written as *Ximistiyo*. According to local tribesmen, this was an area which harboured large and dense swarms; the north–eastern monsoon wind would eventually carry the swarms southwards, where they would breed on a vast scale.

During my reconnaissance, I was surprised to find out that the usage of the word 'Gu' has two meanings by tribes who inhabited areas which were adjacent to one another. 'Gu' usually means 'spring'; however, at least one tribe uses the word to denote 'summer'. When one recorded what one believed to be concrete information relating to when locusts bred in certain areas, then conflicting meanings of the same word by different Somali tribes resulted in apparent contradiction. During my second reconnaissance, such confusion was clarified.

At last, I reached the lighthouse at the tip of the Horn. Alfredo embraced me. He asked me if I 'was just passing by'? I asked Alfredo how many visitors he had received since we had last met four years previously. Alfredo looked thoughtful for a moment. He looked at me, smiling just a little. Then he responded, "One."

Dear Reader, I hope we have not spent too long in the World of the Desert Locust. I suggest we should now look at some aspects of another world, namely, the World of Sleeping Sickness.

FOUR

LIVING IN THE UGANDAN WORLD OF SLEEPING SICKNESS

Up to now, my short stories have centred on the desert locust. Now we can put these stories behind us and concentrate instead on an altogether different African affliction, namely sleeping sickness; its scientific name is *trypanosomiasis*.

After the abrupt abolition of Desert Locust Control in early 1962, the Administrator of the East African Community, Mr. Dunstan Omari, offered me an array of posts, from which any one I could choose. I chose to undertake the administrative and financial management to run the East African Trypanomiasis Research Organization (EATRO) in Tororo, Uganda. EATRO had a staff of about 450, who supported the research work of 12 scientists. These worked in such fields as medicine, immunology, entomology and biochemistry.

In this story, I will explain the key elements of the sleeping sickness disease. With appreciation, I readily acknowledge the information provided to me by the World Health Organization (WHO). This will be followed by a description of developments which forced us to leave a peaceful country, a country which found itself plunged into horrific chaos and tyranny, where anarchy and misery became the order of the day.

I would like to emphasise that I am now writing about the period in the early sixties, before enormous efforts were introduced to fully understand the nature of sleeping sickness, *trypanosomiasis*. I mention this point because the situation today in terms of the occurrence of the disease is quite different to the situation some 60 years ago.

The disease is caused by being bitten by a vector–borne protozoa called the *trypanosome*, of which there are a number of strains. Often, the *trypanosome* infects the tsetse fly, which in turn bites human beings. The control of the tsetse fly was a quite different problem to the control of the desert locust. First, tsetse flies are not found in gregarious swarms and, second, they do not roost on the top of leaves or branches, but underneath in the shade. From an aerial spraying point of view, therefore, it would be extremely difficult, virtually impossible, to devise techniques which would find the target roosting underneath the leaves of trees.

I recall a project which aimed to clear the African bush, to the extent that the tsetse fly could no longer survive without shade. The project failed due to its high costs and the fact that regeneration was quite rapid, especially once the rainy season started.

Although organisations, such as the World Health Organisation (WHO), have spearheaded information–gathering and the compilation of statistics on sleeping sickness, in fact, statistics inevitably include an unquantifiable element, simply because of the nature of the transmission of the disease, linked with the fact that there are very large numbers of an African population who contract the disease but do not register at a medical treatment centre.

The physical effects of contracting the disease are extremely unpleasant, since the brain and other organs are affected by degrees, until a person finds himself/herself physically and mentally handicapped. Symptoms vary when they may be found; some sufferers may function as human beings for some years before they become seriously affected by the disease.

Most of the populations affected by sleeping sickness live in rural conditions, or they may maintain their livelihood by animal husbandry, or general agriculture. In fact, very large areas of potential productive agricultural land are effectively closed to human settlement, due to the disease. At the personal level, I recall a journey from western Tanzania to Dar es Salaam in the East, where it was forbidden to drive through the huge area. The authorities concerned requested us to travel using a goods train; this meant that we actually lived on the train for 36 hours.

Concerning diagnosis of the disease, today, this involves serological tests and testing microscopically for the parasite in body fluids. However, having explained this theoretical desirability, little imagination is needed to understand that, in an African country such as Uganda, such a procedure could definitely not be practised on a large scale. So the reality was that very few diseased people registered at a medical centre; and quite possibly, by the time they may have done so, the disease would have been already advanced.

The EATRO medical section usually supported about 12 sleeping sickness patients who were in various stages of the disease. Although these patients were there for research purposes, in fact, a number reacted favourably to forms of treatment which were in the early stages of development. Primarily, the patients were subjected to virtually constant observation, accompanied by clinical tests. This research work enabled suitable drugs to be developed at a latest stage, drugs which would combat to some extent the disease.

In order for *trypanosomiasis* research to be undertaken internationally, it was essential that trypanosomes were available for experimental purposes. To meet this demand, EATRO maintained a bank of strains of trypanosomes; these were contained in hundreds of capillary tubes and stored in a sophisticated deep–freeze system. The process of isolating and identifying the trypanosomes, centrifuging, placing them in the small capillary tubes, storing them and documenting the various strains required considerable scientific specialised skill and was time–consuming. EATRO was recognised by the World Health Organisation (WHO) for the quality of its research work and, in particular, as a designated source of trypanosomes which could be made available throughout the world for research purposes.

In 1966, as the security situation in Uganda drastically deteriorated, it was recognised that the trypanosomes, so meticulously collected and maintained in the bank, might well be put at risk, even though I had ensured that if the system lost power, a fail–safe generator would immediately start operating.

At about that time, a biochemist decided, on his own initiative, to try and transfer the contents of the bank to Nairobi, a secure location. He would pack a large vacuum flask with dry ice and insert a number of capillary tubes in the flask, which would be placed in a picnic basket. Adriel Njogu would then head for the Kenya border in his car. At the border, he would be challenged by the semi–trained young Ugandan soldiers; the explanation given was that Adriel Njogu would be meeting some friends for a picnic in Kenya. If the soldiers had examined his 'picnic', the consequences for Adriel Njogu could have been unpleasantly serious.

The picnic exercise was repeated on many occasions, until much of the collection of trypanosomes contained in the bank had been transferred to suitable deep–freeze facilities in Nairobi. Thus, trypanosomes continued to be available for research purposes worldwide. Without these efforts, research into sleeping sickness would have been severely curtailed. Mankind owes a considerable debt to the selfless, courageous actions of Adriel Njogu.

Another important activity of EATRO was to examine tsetse flies, many of which were infected with trypanosomes. In order to collect tsetse flies, a group of 40 young men were selected; the members of the group were usually called 'fly boys'. The group was transported for work weekly to a tsetse fly–infested area, near the shore of Lake Victoria.

I regularly visited the fly boys at their work. On one occasion, I paid attention to the quality of sleeping accommodations used by the group. They were sleeping in what were virtually large huts; these were constructed of mud and wattle. The fly boys were vulnerable in the sense that there was no protection against mosquitoes, so they were certainly vulnerable to malaria, a killing disease. Before leaving the area, I asked the group of fly boys to meet me for a discussion.

In pursuing the discussion with the group of fly boys, with some difficulty I obtained their agreement to build a new complex close to their existing accommodation. Initially, they did not agree; to my surprise, the fly boys stated they were quite happy with the rooms in the large huts at their disposal and they had no wish to see the existing accommodation replaced by a new, upgraded complex.

This was one of several examples where one found it difficult to help those who are poor. To raise the level of the poor is not an easy task, as many would believe it to be. Poor people become accustomed to their condition and they often have a tendency to suspect those who promise improvements.

However compassionate one may feel towards the poor, they themselves often express a feeling of security in the condition of poverty. This seems to be illogical, but it is often the case; they would need to be satisfied that it was an improvement on their precondition. In fact, when the new complex was ready, the fly boys took little time in reaching the conclusion that the new accommodation was a great improvement on the existing premises. In contrast to the older premises, the new complex was mosquito–proof and bathroom facilities were also available; none had existed in the old premises.

Personal and domestic aspects of life in Uganda in the early sixties was a scene which changed from peaceful tranquillity to horrendous, tragic chaos and tyranny.

EATRO had been built about six miles from the small town of Tororo, itself situated quite close to the border with Kenya. Most of the staff were housed closed by. It was, in any case, mandatory for the director and myself to live in the vicinity; we lived a few hundred metres from EATRO. The group of houses was isolated, although the surroundings were pleasantly green. One looked over an expansive, shallow valley, which supported two thousand cattle; they were available for experimental purposes. Sleeping sickness occurs in cattle; in Uganda, it is called *Nagana.*

For the first two years of our four-year stay in Uganda, we felt that we were living in a make–believe 'Shangri–La'. The serenity and tranquillity of the Ugandans extended to such a degree that it seemed unreal; these were happy, contented people. By western standards, most were relatively poor; on the other hand, they grew bananas and cash crops (such as cotton or coffee) and the climate was pleasantly warm. The people showed no envy of those who were materially better off; and their appearance never approached that of the wretched, poverty–stricken very poor who, for example, have the misfortune to live in the slums of big cities. The missionary influence in Uganda generally was strong and, at the time that independence was declared in 1962, the country as a whole was developing steadily and well.

Several industries had been established. Tourism was a major foreign exchange earner; the Uganda game parks were well–run and offered wonderful opportunities to view a rich and vast array of African wildlife. The Kilembe copper mines in the foothills of the Ruwenzori Mountain Ranger (the so–called Mountains of the Moon) were highly productive; other industrial ventures based on mining showed considerable promise. Uganda cotton was an excellent cash crop and brought healthy profits, through co–operative schemes, to the growers. Plantations established for the growing and processing of tea, coffee and sugar were well–run and productive.

The foundation of good public services had also been laid. The Jinja hydroelectric scheme on the Victoria Nile (the Owen Falls Dam) was a success of far–reaching significance. En passant, the Victoria Nile is the longest river in the world. The Makerere University College symbolised the excellence of the educational system.

In 1963, I wrote a letter to a friend in England. I told him of the dynamic advances which had been made in various ways within Uganda. These were indeed impressive. But I tempered the account with what I saw as a reality: the situation which had been created by the progress made was, essentially, fragile. For example, I recounted that one could well be impressed with the quality of the highway between Tororo and Kampala, a drive of a hundred and thirty miles. But if one stopped along the way and walked into the bush, one would soon reach the conclusion that development still had some way to go, if it were to be firmly established. Away from the main towns, or the main transport arteries, rural life in the villages did not seem to have been positively touched by the benefits of the development.

Two or three years later, the overall political picture was changing rapidly. The Kabaka (King Freddie) had been overthrown and had fled to England to spend his last days helping the poor in the East End of London. In order to sustain his position, Milton Obote, the prime minister, increasingly relied on the support of the army. The commanding officer was not prepared to give his full co–operation and he was placed under arrest and summarily dealt with. Eventually, the successor who emerged and, in fact, would later seize power was one Idi Amin.

Before the terror overtook Uganda in 1966, we made numerous excursions to the game parks which had been established and which had proved to be so popular with tourists. In addition, we walked up Mount Elgon (14,000 feet) and made several excursions to Karamoja, an area in the north eastern part of Uganda. The Karamajong tribesmen were indeed distinctive; most were scantily clad and many carried their bows and arrows for daily hunting.

It was during one of our weekend excursions in Karamoja that we stopped in a forest area in the foothills of Mount Elgon. We were struck by the beauty of the forest, the birdlife and the quality of the light as the sun's rays were dispersed by the leaves of the huge trees. We were surprised to suddenly hear some voices; we had thought that we were quite alone. I wandered through the dense undergrowth in the direction of the voices and, peering through the thick foliage, I saw an extraordinary sight. A group of about fifty men were being drilled in how to

Eastern Uganda – a man from yet another World
He is vulnerable to sleeping sickness

handle firearms. The men were dressed in semi–rags and, as they performed various parts of their drills, they made aggressive noises. I had no doubt that they were involved in an illegal activity and I felt that the sooner we could separate ourselves from them, the better. What they would have done with me had they seen me, I did not know; I felt apprehensive.

In contrast to the serenity of the pre–Idi Amin period, the Uganda we had so enjoyed had changed. Almost daily, we were reminded that the security situation was degenerating. One day, returning from meetings from Nairobi, at the border crossing from Kenya into Uganda, I was mildly (although unpleasantly) manhandled and the armed immigration personnel were rude and abusive.

Meanwhile, although the EATRO staff continued to go about their business with efficiency, all were aware that the security situation was declining steadily. During the following weeks, a number of incidents reminded many of us of our physical vulnerability.

Some days before finally leaving Tororo, yet another incident occurred. In the East African context, it contained the ingredients of incongruous humour, irony, tragedy and (at least to me) an element of unpredictable pantomime.

We awoke one morning to a brilliantly clear day; typically, it had rained heavily the previous afternoon. From our house at the end of the row of five, we looked out across our acre of garden. The lawn was heavy with dew and glistened in the sunlight; it was surrounded by beautiful trees and shrubs. Apart from a huge fig tree and two papayas, I noticed a splash of red, which was a hibiscus bush in full flower. Looking over the expansive view which stretched below to the south–east, the definition of the shallow valley was gradually lost in a blue haze which seemed to hang over the flourishing trees along the sides of the small river. Behind the house, we looked across undulating bush land and low trees; beyond were the Sukulu hills, which were a few hundred feet high.

As I left for the office, I turned to Emy (my darling wife) and waved; every morning of my working life, Emy waved me goodbye. On this occasion, her happy smile perfectly reflected the idyllic surroundings. Although the half–mile drive was short, I could not avoid thinking about the tragedy of degradation which was beginning to overtake Uganda. The people were so contented; they did not deserve the civil unrest which was beginning to take hold in the country. An hour or so after my arrival at the office, I answered a telephone call; to my surprise, Emy was on the line.

Emy said, "Are you busy? I mean, do you have time to talk for a moment?" In view of what Emy then said, I can only comment that she was remarkably controlled and calm. "I thought I should ring you, because our house is surrounded with soldiers." However busy I might have been, thank goodness I had had time to talk! I ran up the corridor to the main entrance of EATRO and drove the half-mile to our house. Indeed, around our house there were soldiers crawling through the bush, crouching or running in stooped fashion from one bush to another; and they were all armed! I jumped over the garden wire fence and approached one of the crawling soldiers. "Would you please tell me what you are doing?" I pleaded.

"We are attacking that house!"

I asked him where his commander might be and was told that the platoon commander could be found under some trees nearby, towards the Sukulu Hills. I then briefly explained that my wife and children were at home and it would be helpful if the attack could be delayed for at least an hour. The commander was soon found; he was a good-looking, young lieutenant. He was sitting on a log, a sub-machine gun at his side, with a mobile radio in front of him; he seemed a little surprised to see me at that particular juncture.

I introduced myself and explained that I lived with my family in the house, which was, apparently, an objective for military attack. The young man glanced at me politely and then spoke in impeccable English; his accent was slightly affected, as though he might have attended one of the older English universities, or perhaps Sandhurst.

"My dear Mr. Everard, I am frightfully sorry that you have been inconvenienced by our military exercise. You see, my dear fellow, the present situation in Uganda is politically rather unstable; perhaps that is an understatement, don't you think? And we have this chap Idi Amin who seems to be throwing his weight about; well, apart from his experience as our heavyweight boxing champion, I couldn't really say whether he is ideally suited for his present job as commander–in–chief of the army. In any event, he is not sure at the moment whether the army will be loyal to him, especially as he has locked up the army commander, General Opolot. So, you see, he has spread the army to the four corners of Uganda, in fragmented fashion, just to ensure temporary military impotence until the situation becomes clearer; quite a good idea, don't you think?

"In any case, it gives chaps like me a problem; how do I keep my men occupied? Well, I thought, why not have a field exercise and attack that house; of course, if there is opposition to be overcome, this makes it that more realistic."

While he was explaining the position in cultured tones, with his sub–machine gun sweeping the air as his arms swayed back and forth, I could not help feeling the irony of the situation. Here was a man who, apparently, had been trained in England; he and his men were armed with British firearms and the cost of their battledress was probably financed by a British taxpayers' subvention to his government. And here was an Englishman, whose house would soon be attacked, with the possibility of his family and himself being sacrificed on the altar of – what, precisely? Was it irony; was it some twisted sort of revenge? I was becoming more confused by the second.

Then I had a brainwave. After thanking the young officer for explaining the situation so clearly, I told him that it could be rather dangerous for our family if the attack were pursued, but, of course, I fully appreciated the position and it was important that the field exercise should be properly completed! I wondered if I might make a small suggestion?

"My dear sir, in the military, we are always open to suggestions – but of course." We had a neighbour (whom I knew was on holiday with his family); might it not be possible to change the objective and attack the neighbour's house? "I must say, I find that an excellent idea. We shall see how the men respond to changed orders!"

As a feeling of cautious relief began to seep into my brain, there was a blare on his field radio. The lieutenant listened intently with his hands pressed against his headset; then he said, "Wilco – out!" He looked at me and said he had just received instructions for the platoon to move immediately. I wondered what this meant and, in particular, whether he and his men would simply move to another location within the vicinity.

"Is your destination far?" I asked as quietly and innocently as possible. The lieutenant was just about to reply, but at the last second, he seemed consciously to close his mouth. Then he looked at me with a look of slight distrust on his face. Then he simply dismissed my question.

"Top secret!"

As the soldiers were being recalled, I walked back to our house. In accordance with our quickly arranged plan, my wife and children had already left for friends, where they stayed for the night just in case another military visitation occurred. I returned to the office, apologising for my absence. A colleague asked me if everything was all right.

"Yes, thank you; it was nothing much. I just had to sort out a small incident." Soon it would be time to leave and I for one would be happy to transfer to the stability of Kenya.

About a week before our departure, one evening we played what would be our last nine holes of golf at the Tororo Club. We would look back on many enjoyable competitions and friendly matches on the compact nine–hole golf course. During the week, one usually played between 5 and 6:30p.m., since by 6:45 or so, dusk fell.

We followed the usual return route to our house and shortly after we had left the main road route on to the dirt (murram) road which would bring us to our house, we were confronted by a road block. As I stopped and lowered my window, a Ugandan soldier approached me, a sub–machine gun hanging from his shoulder. I said, "Good evening."

The soldier glared at me and responded, "You are a very rude man!" I smiled gently and explained that I had simply said, good evening; perhaps I should have said: *Hujambo, Bwana*!

The soldier said, "You are not only a very rude man, now you are arguing!"

It was clear that the man was in a nervous state and, as he was beginning to gesticulate with his sub–machine gun, I decided to keep quiet. I did not answer and waited for his next move. We only had to wait a few seconds. The soldier said, "All of you; out of the car. I'm going to search it."

Emy, our children and I left the car and stood in a group close by. I turned to Emy and said, "I am terribly sorry that this has happened. I was hoping that before there were any more incidents, we would have left the country. It is one thing for a man to take risks on his own account; but I should have arranged earlier for you and the children to have left. I am so sorry!"

After the soldier had completed his peremptory search of

our car, he stood in front of me and seemed to be in a state of extreme agitation. His right hand swept his automatic weapon from side to side fairly quickly; his forefinger was outstretched, although I could not precisely see in the half–light whether his finger covered the trigger guard, or the trigger itself. His eyes flashing, he blurted out, "You are a lucky man. Now I will let you go, but if you ever come this way again and you are rude, things will be very different!"

Feeling weak, but relieved, we slowly drove home.

The same evening, I organized things for the following morning. At 6a.m., a truck appeared in front of our house. A small group of labourers helped us to load the truck with most of our selected belongings. After three hours, the truck left for its destination in Kenya. We followed shortly after.

We never returned to Uganda.

Looking back on our four years' sojourn in Uganda, we remembered delightful people, a landscape which varied from the semi–desert of Karamoja to the luxuriant forest of the foothills of the Ruwenzori Mountains, the concentrations of wildlife in the parks, the warm climate (which was sometimes interrupted by dramatic electrical storms of incredible intensity), and a period of productive work. The work aspect seemed to be a period of personal re–adjustment, in preparation for a change of career orientation.

En passant, the British statesman Sir Winston Churchill visited parts of Africa, including Uganda, in the early 1900s. In 1908, his book *My African Journey* was published. He wrote:

> *"For magnificence, for variety of form and color, for profusion of brilliant life — bird, insect, reptile, beast — for vast scale — Uganda is truly 'the Pearl of Africa.'"*

We also would never forget those isolated, unpleasant incidents; these had harshly reminded us that we were living in a country which had gradually degenerated until it would become savagely ravaged as a result of the crazed actions of a handful of misguided, selfish, anarchic political leaders. That so many owed so much misery to so few represents one of the worst blots on what should have been (without their efforts) one of the most successful stories of social and industrial development in recent African history.

STORIES OF ASIA

FIVE

THE WORLD OF AIR SAFETY IN ASIA

Almost fifty years ago, on an incredibly cold, windy winter's day when the temperature dipped to -23C., I arrived in Montreal in Canada; I had arrived to take up my appointment with the International Civil Aviation Organization (ICAO). The section I was to head was there to provide logistical support (in the widest sense) for some 200 air safety projects which were under implementation in rather more than 100 developing (Third World) countries.

The International Civil Aviation Organization (ICAO) was established a few years after the end of WW2. Even before the end of hostilities, there was recognition that rules would need to be agreed on if the aviation industry, including airlines, would develop in an orderly way.

The role of ICAO was to spearhead air safety rules to assure international air navigation safety. ICAO was established by the *Convention on International Civil Aviation.* Virtually all countries of the world (193 countries) have signed what is usually called *The Chicago Convention*. ICAO has a governing council with members drawn from the international community. The organization comprises bureaux, or divisions. As part of the many aviation–related activities of ICAO, I would like to highlight two important functions.

First, signatories to the convention must comply with ICAO's standards. If a country cannot comply with a standard, then the country must send to ICAO a so–called Notice of Difference. In addition to its standards, ICAO issues recommended practices; although these are not mandatory, they are normally expected to be followed.

Second, although a handful of developed countries constantly spearhead ways and means to improve flight safety, at the same time, ICAO fully recognises that developing (Third World) countries often meet almost insuperable challenges: these may include financial constraints or, perhaps, lack of infrastructure, whether this may involve lack of human trained and experienced personnel, or properly equipped buildings and facilities.

For the next 12 years, I worked as hard as I knew how in overseeing ICAO air safety projects in Asia (and the Pacific). Apart from the government (or its civil aviation agency) meeting half of the cost of a project, the remaining cost needed to be financed. So, in order to support the government's efforts, I soon became familiar with the workings of, for instance, the World Bank, the Development Banks, the UN Development Programme, the Iraqi Development Fund, the OPEC Fund, and so forth. And I had to learn the ins and outs of financing.

One also needed to be aware of certain Asian customs which were different to those practised in the western civilization. Although most of these were minor, the fact that a westerner had learned particular customs was appreciated. In Asia, generally, one shows the utmost courtesy; one should also learn the way a greeting is expressed, usually with the hands, rarely verbally. In some countries, it is impolite to point a foot directly at a person, especially someone at close hand.

Then we have the custom of what is often termed 'Face'. In Europe, normally we have little problem in accepting our faults;

personally, when a mistake occurs in work with which I might be associated, the first person I consider is myself. In contrast, in Asia this approach is rarely found; one should avoid losing 'Face'.

To illustrate this point, I recall our organization overseeing significant renovation work at an airport. During the work period, the contactor's team cut an electrical cable. Part of the consequence was that our resident engineer could not work after about 6.30 in the early evening, when the light faded.

When I made a visit to the airport and was told about the problem, I asked for an appointment with the airport manager. The next day, I was duly received and related the vain attempts of our resident engineer to have the cable repaired for immediate operation. I was curtly dismissed, with a denial from the manager that he could do absolutely nothing; he had no intention in becoming involved in other people's business!

The following day, I again visited the airport. The resident engineer was smiling with delight – yes, the cable had been repaired and the electrical system was functioning perfectly.

Yes, dear Reader, this little story illustrates 'Face', an attitude that is widespread in many Asian (and some African) countries.

Being a strong believer in eyeball to eyeball discussions, I travelled frequently and extensively. I soon became familiar with the civil aviation top management in the People's Republic of China, North Korea, Viet Nam, Thailand, Bangladesh, Bhutan, Myanmar, Nepal, Pakistan, Sri Lanka, Maldives, Indonesia, Philippines, Papua New Guinea, and so forth.

All of these countries had fine people managing the civil aviation systems. However, all were very conscious of failings and weaknesses. And they looked to ICAO for assistance. They could all rely on me, on behalf of ICAO, to do our practical level best to support them. It was all very hard work.

Although we worked and worked, there was still time for an element of humour; a civil aviation director general comes to mind. He was an affable person; and when I entered his office for our scheduled meeting, he used to shake my hand and say, "Always good to see you, Colin, we have a lot to discuss. We should strengthen ourselves for the long haul. The usual?" Without waiting for my response, he pressed a button.

Shortly afterwards, an immaculately attired servant, dressed in spotless white with a brilliant red sash, would enter carrying a large tray, which was placed on the somewhat grandiose desk. Apart from cakes and biscuits, there were two cups and saucers and a large pot of tea, resting on the tray; all were of elegant, beautiful English porcelain. Without more ado, my host would take hold of the teapot. Then, with a wry smile and muttering, "This will strengthen us," he poured from the lovely teapot. Invariably, he poured a little neat whisky!

Perhaps it might be enlightening if we pause a little and give thought to the size of the huge challenge which exists in our world concerning the difference between a developed country and the rest of the world.

Of the world's number of countries, about 15 are called 'developed' countries. This leaves a balance of about 178 countries which constitute the 'developing' countries. The UN classifies these countries as Newly Industrialized Countries (NICs), Least Developed Countries (LDCs), and the rest.

Of the developing countries, 46 are classified as 'Least Developed'; many of these are countries of Africa. In Asia, several countries fall in the LDC classification; these include Bangladesh, Bhutan, Nepal, Maldives and Myanmar.

The UN describes the characteristics of a developing country as follows:

> *A developing country is a country with a relatively low standard of living, undeveloped industrial base, and moderate to low Human Development Index (HDI). This index is a comparative measure of poverty, literacy, education, life expectancy, and other factors for countries worldwide.*

The UN describes, separately, the characteristics of a Least Developed Country; many LDCs have a per capita *annual* income which equates to a little over US$1,000! Dear Reader, with deep respect, may I invite you to meditate on the type of impact which such a situation produces; we are considering the everyday fate of literally billions of human beings.

In my last book, I described a situation which, in my opinion, reflected the reality of those in our world who are very poor. I wrote:

'At one point I noticed ahead what seemed to be an amorphous heap of dark grey and brown; perhaps they were rags. As I drew closer to the shapeless heap, I realised that the heap was inhabited by a small woman, who apparently was in deep slumber. I thought she was almost certainly ill; perhaps she was suffering from malaria, I thought. As far as her belongings were concerned she had none, although a small, dirty–looking kettle rested near her head; the kettle was without a lid and a little water glistened slightly in the sunshine.

'I knelt down beside the motionless creature and gently felt her forehead. Within a second the woman opened her eyes. With a shocked shriek, she raised her head, took hold of the handle of the kettle and hugged it in her bosom. Glaring at me, suddenly she swung the kettle as fast as she was able; the swing came to an abrupt end as the kettle hit my head. Astonished at her reaction, and with a wet head, I withdrew and continued my walk.

'This was a woman who typified the low end of the spectrum of wealth in our world. Many of us have the privilege of living in a so–called developed part of the world where human beings can, and do, amass seemingly endless wealth. And then we have the vast less developed part of the world, where millions of human beings live in wretched, abject poverty, like that woman. She carried with her what for her was a very valuable piece of property; this was her dirty kettle. It could well have been her only property; and she was afraid I wanted to steal her possession!'

At the other end of the UN list of developing countries is a small group of so–called Newly Industrialized Countries. In Asia, these include India, Indonesia, Malaysia, Philippines, Pakistan, Singapore and Thailand.

In the context of air safety, what are the types of problems facing developing (Third World) countries?

Typically, in most developing countries, the basic problem centres on lack of finance. And when one considers that financing to improve a country's civil aviation infrastructure needs to compete, for example, with finance earmarked for education or health, then it becomes self–evident that civil aviation administrations face a challenging task.

The training and retention of specialized personnel presents a major challenge. Especially in Asia in the 1980s, civil aviation was expanding at about 10 per cent each year in terms of passengers and freight carried. In turn, such fields as air traffic management or communications engineering were constantly expanding. Personnel problems were sometimes exacerbated due to other, richer, countries offering trained staff to leave their home country to work, with greatly increased remuneration, in the richer country.

Communications engineering is another important field where only properly qualified and experienced staff are essential if sophisticated civil aviation equipment and systems are to function reliably.

To help fill infrastructure failings, ICAO projects helped a great deal. Normally, a project contained elements of expertise, equipment and training; so these projects were a means of bringing expertise from the developed into the developing world. The ultimate aim of a project was to terminate it as soon as possible, leaving behind a functioning infrastructure of national personnel.

During the crucially important period of the 1980s and early '90s, Asian civil aviation authorities weathered the storm of lack of comprehensive infrastructure in the best way possible. ICAO's support was vital, given the circumstances. Only one member state recorded significant failing vis à vis ICAO Standards. With the agreement of the government, ICAO assumed responsibility to assure proper adherence to ICAO Standards. Over three years of formal and practical training, the country concerned was able to take over the reins again.

In the mid 1980s, I found myself at home preparing for yet another mission to Asia. All arrangements were in place for my official visits to China, North Korea, Cambodia, Thailand, Bangladesh, Nepal and Pakistan. I left our home in Montreal on a summer's day. By now, my wife and our children had become accustomed to the father of the household leaving on his travels; usually, I would be away from home for about a month or so.

On this occasion, as I left home, I found children playing together in the sunshine, just outsider our front door. Each child was holding a little clay pipe. Resting on a parapet, for the use of the children, was a bowl of soapy, frothy water. Then the children would fill their pipes and blow bubbles above their heads into the atmosphere. The scene of blowing bubbles was a pretty one. Then I noticed that as the bubbles floated upwards, the rays of the sun shone on them; the result was beautiful. The bubbles took on the lovely colours of a rainbow, as they floated upwards against the background of the azure of the sky.

Then I left. With the Canadian Pacific airline, I took the five–hour flight to Vancouver; then, after a wait of two hours, we were on the fifteen-hours trans-Pacific flight to Tokyo. The following day, my mission began.

Although these missions were exhausting, both mentally and physically (as the representative of ICAO, in the meeting room I was expected to authoritatively know more than anyone else present!), at the same time, I often found my visits to be full of inspiration. Why? Because the men and women who work in international civil aviation belong (consciously or unconsciously) to a fraternity. This is a simple fact.

A highly qualified engineer, for instance, in Nepal may be earning less than US$150 a month. But, day or night, he will spring into action to ensure the operational perfection of the navigational aids required to assure safe landings. In order to survive, many of these top professional people have perhaps three jobs; in addition to their designated job, they pursue other work in their spare time.

I recall once visiting an air traffic control tower at a provincial airport in India. The shade temperature was 42 degrees C. With the airport manager as my courteous escort, I climbed the steps of the tower. Once inside, I chatted with the sole air traffic controller; he was full of good humour. After a few minutes, I felt I was being overcome by the stuffy heat. "You look a bit pale, Mr. Everard. Yes, it's quite warm in here – almost 50 degrees. I have a glass of water here, but it's not for you – too dirty; we are used to dirt! Sit down. Try not to pass out – we will organise a bottle of clean water in five minutes."

I subsequently raised the question of air conditioning with the airport manager. My question was dismissed. "No money for luxuries!"

"So, how long is his shift?" I asked.

"Six hours."

"And do you mind me asking, please, what does an air traffic controller earn in these parts?" The number was the equivalent of US$75 per month.

As I have written, wherever you may meet civil aviation people in developing countries, these professionals are poorly remunerated – yet, they are members of a fraternity which is dedicated to perfection in the interest of air safety.

And when you have the privilege of working with these dedicated professionals, they become nothing less than inspirational.

A few years ago, in Nice, I presented a paper to the 1,000-strong International Congress of the Aeronautical Sciences. For just a few days, I was so happy to be, and feel, that I was a member of the aviation fraternity. In the spirit of the fraternity, it was a pleasure to feel 'part of it' again. And I enjoyed being somewhat spoiled by the president and his colleagues!

Now I was doing my best in Pakistan, the last country of my mission. I had meetings in both Islamabad (where, unexpectedly, I met the president of Pakistan, General Mohamed Zia-ul-Haq), and in Karachi. In Karachi, at the final meeting, I had agreed that I would draft a project document for funding approval by the UN Development Programme. The document would be handed over the following morning at the airport just before my departure. So, of course, I had a full night's work ahead of me.

On entering my hotel, the Avari Tower, I was handed a message. It was from ICAO in Montreal. Although I had visited Bangladesh for three days, apparently, the minister of transport wished to discuss an urgent matter of consequence. I replied (in those days using telex) that I was at the end of my mission and would be leaving for London and Montreal the next day. I suggested that the head of ICAO's Regional Office in Bangkok should contact the minister and arrange to visit Bangladesh. I then put the matter out of my mind.

After working all night, at 6a.m. the following morning, I was ready to leave for the airport. I had prepared the 15–page project document, which would be handed over at the airport. As I was about to leave the hotel, a man from the reception hurried towards me; he was carrying a message. The message stated that the Bangladeshi minister insisted that only I should meet him; I noticed that Colin Everard was typed in block capital letters.

Later that day, I embarked for the flight to Dhaka. Although I was extremely fatigued, I had to cope with the flight time of at least 9 hours. Three days later, at last I could head for home – which way should I travel? I opted for the trans-Pacific route. So I took a flight to Bangkok, where the ICAO Office organized my journey to Montreal. The distance from Bangkok is about 8,000 miles, or 13,000 kilometres.

As mentioned, the trans-Pacific flight from Tokyo has a duration of about fifteen hours. Depending on the upper air winds, this duration could vary; I recall one flight when, after 17 hours of the aircraft's speed being reduced by strong headwinds, the captain became concerned due to the possibility he might run out of fuel.

Shortly after take–off from Tokyo, I began my routine of dictating what we called 'mission reports'. On my return to Montreal, these would be transcribed by the section's secretaries. En passant, although I was overseeing and helping to coordinate the work of 75 project managers in Asia and the Pacific, the section's staff in Montreal numbered only about 10 (including 4 secretaries); we were of 7 nationalities. Part of ICAO's culture was to expend the minimum on administrative staff; this approach was strongly applied in our Technical Cooperation Bureau. As a generalization, ICAO was sometimes referred to as 'lean and mean'.

After dictating two mission reports, I began to realise that what I was doing did not coincide with my usual routine. Instead of speaking clearly, I found myself hesitating while my memory was groping for what I wanted to explain. Then I noticed that a short stutter sometimes intervened in my dictation. So I paused and I looked out of the window; as a distraction, I tried to take in the limitless expanse of the Pacific Ocean. Then I fell asleep.

"Do you feel all right, sir?" It was a friendly flight attendant. "You look quite pale. You've flown with us before – I saw you at least twice," she continued. Then I ate a meal – the choice was usually chicken or pasta. Now, I thought, you can have a good sleep. Unfortunately, however, this proved to be impossible. I seemed to be sleepy, but at the same time, I was awake. Then I started meditating – and what did I see in my thoughts?

I saw children blowing bubbles, just outside our front door in Montreal. And then I saw scenes of our children, with their mother and myself, as my wife Emy and I were progressing through our married life.

Suddenly, although quietly, I heard myself reciting a little poem.

Eventually, when I had returned to Montreal, I retrieved the memory of sitting in that aircraft reciting a poem; mentally, at that time, I seemed to be bordering a state of dreaming, or perhaps even hallucination. In any case, with the poem in my brain, I thought I should write it down. The poem takes the form of two sonnets.

This is what I wrote (for convenience, the poem is written on the following page):

THE BUBBLE OF LOVE

Or Reflections On A Mature Conjugal Relationship

I dream – I feel that love is like a bubble,
It dances, and laughs, in sun–kissed rays of hope,
Is it real, or illusory – clear of trouble?
Yes, it has colours of the rainbow, floats,
Shimmering in the breeze. This bubble is love.
Caressed by warm bodies in consummation
Love rests lightly on the wings of a dove,
At night a veritable constellation.
This bubble reflects only affection
Beautifully, like a myriad of stars.
Development, nourishment, attention
Steer your bubble on glittering paths.
As a maxim, strive hard for creation
Of a true partnership of rock–like foundation.

Neglect your bubble? Accept the certainty
All hell will unleash; your bubble will burst
Degenerating into enmity,
First producing volatility, later, worse,
Sterility towards that loved one for whom
You once professed everlasting devotion
With glorious adoration; and which soon
Became passionately conceived perfection.
Take the advice of those in the know.
Stay true to the end and reap your harvest
Of maturing love with increasing glow,
Ever plumbing new depths, till your final rest.
This is the right way to avoid trouble
Living in love – through a radiant bubble.

The psychology of exhaustion is unfathomably fascinating – I think you will agree!

SIX

A SHINING BEACON IN THE WORLD OF THE INDIAN CASTE SYSTEM

For much of the substance of this story, I must acknowledge with deep, heartfelt thanks the advice and help of Professor Anuradha Sivaraman (University of Delaware, USA).

Dear Reader, I hope I still have your interest? This story is disparate in the context of the collection as a whole; although I have visited different parts of India over a period of some fifteen years, in contrast to all of the other stories, this is a story of which I have little direct, personal experience. Nevertheless, I believe you will agree that the subject matter (as I have described it in the above story title), is of great interest to us all. I, for one, have found that background information I have read is enlightening.

Geographically, the shape of India roughly resembles the shape of a triangle, with its broadest part on top – that is the northern part. From west to east in the north would mean a road journey of some two thousand kilometres. From north to south, the distance is rather more than three thousand kilometres.

In this story, after a concise description of the Indian caste system, I aim to describe a human being who, one might say, 'broke the rules' and became an intellectual beacon of human achievement, in the widest sense of the word. So now, without more ado, let us understand some of the tenets of the Indian caste system.

At an early stage in its very long history, ancient India developed a caste system which was based solely on professions; these dovetailed successfully with other castes. There were seven castes. These were called: the Sages, the Tillers of the Soil / Husbandmen, the Herdsmen, the Handicraftsmen and Retail Dealers, the Warriors, the Superintendents, and the Councilors of the State.

At a later juncture, there were five social classes to which families belonged, from the *Brahmins* at the top to the *Dalit* ("Untouchables") at the bottom. At that time, although the *Dalit* were not considered part of the caste system, their role in society was determined by their being literal outcasts. Below, I have briefly commented on the *Dalit* people.

Today, there are about three thousand Indian castes, with literally thousands of sub-castes. The population of India is about 1.4 billion; of this number, rather more than one hundred and forty million people belong to the lowest caste, the so–called Untouchables.

As I have written, the *Dalit* (to the extent they are still recognised as such), have virtually no rights as citizens. From the day of their birth, they need to come to terms with their lack of status in Indian society. An unquantifiable number still lead wretched lives, in poverty. Fortunately, over the last hundred years or so, significant political progress has been made to improve the status of the *Dalit*; however, much remains to be done.

In an article published by National Geographic in 2003, concerning progress in the emancipation of *Dalits*, the overall picture which is presented is bleak, sometimes graphically horrifying. The authors write of widespread human rights abuses against *Dalits* and lack of literacy on a very large scale. The principle part of the *Dalits*' rejection by other castes is the lack of enforcement of laws; this situation is critically made worse by widespread, deeply held religious beliefs. Most countries in our world suffer from intractable problems affecting their populations. It is sad that India suffers in this respect more than most.

National legislation has been enacted to nullify the very low status of these human beings, the *Dalit*. But a system which has existed for at least three thousand years cannot be nullified by the stroke of a presidential pen; to set aside the ancient lineage of the Untouchables will certainly need long–term, continued, well–planned and co–ordinated, persistent action, which itself will take time.

As an outsider, I would like to make the point that while few could exaggerate the complexity of the Indian caste system, the basic concept of establishing and maintaining a hierarchical social order is certainly not new. In ancient Europe, for example, in medieval France and Spain, such a system was enforced. Or, today, in the Kingdom of Bhutan, many wear a coloured sash, denoting the social rank of the holder. And no one is permitted to use the colour yellow, which is reserved for the use of His Majesty the King.

Then again, there are countries which profess to practice democracy, where unwritten laws prevail; often, the understanding of certain 'unwritten' laws lead to appointments of members of only a highly exclusive group, who have a specific social position. Of course, probably few of the instances given apply their hierarchical rules as strictly as is to be found in the Indian caste system.

In summary, the caste system is a division of people into distinct groups based on occupation or lineage. A caste system is a type of society built on a hierarchy of supposed worthiness. Cultural purity is an attribute assigned to a group or individuals. The list of groups is very long; the list includes intellectual achievement, the accumulation of wealth through employing good business practices and ethics, and so forth. Each of the levels has its own rights and obligations; these decrease down the hierarchy, ending with the lowest level, which has no rights at all. The members of this Untouchable level are often regarded as outcast criminals.

The caste system inherently supports marriage between two members of the same societal level. Caste systems are designed to protect the cultural purity of the hierarchal levels from each other, and its society in general from external influences. Cultural purity means that a culture (i.e., Hinduism) continues and does not reconcile itself with other cultures which interact with its adherents (i.e., Buddhism or Daoism). From an economic standpoint, caste systems provide the societal framework for an efficient and tightly controlled, closed system, which supports internal economic growth while maintaining isolationism.

India is the most striking and enduring example of a nation that is imbued with a caste system.

The 1950 Constitution of India includes steps not only to improve the lot of the Untouchables, the Constitution actually bans Untouchability. However, the lineage remains; this is sometimes culturally used to show discrimination against the supposedly former Untouchables. In other words, the cultural approach prevails, as practiced during the very long Indian civilization. So, although there is quite definitely progress in adhering to the provisions of the Indian Constitution, the practice of discrimination against *Dalits* lives on.

I now invite you, dear Reader, to accompany me along the way to the remarkable end of this story. It focuses on a man who, as a *Dalit*, rose from the quagmire of his fellow human beings and, against all the odds, reached the political pinnacle of the whole country. The name of this Dalit was Bhimrao Ramji Ambedkar.

For much of the substance which follows, I wish to acknowledge, with thanks, the information provided by the *Encyclopaedia Britannica*.

Ambedkar was born a *Dalit* in 1891, in western India. His father was an officer in the Indian Army. Born a *Dalit*, at school he was treated badly by pupils of higher castes; sometimes, he was even humiliated by groups of fellow pupils.

Apparently, he cast aside his inborn handicap and strongly pursued his academic studies. His achievements were brought

Bhimrao Ramji Ambedkar – A shining beacon in the history of India.

to the attention of the Ruler of Baroda. who was so deeply impressed that the ruler extended an academic scholarship to Ambedkar. This enabled Ambedkar to study further; in fact, Ambedkar studied intensely in the United States of America, the United Kingdom and Germany.

May I suggest that, at this point, we briefly pause to dwell on the fact that these accomplishments were achieved by a *Dalit*, a so–called Untouchable – yes, by a human being who was regarded by other castes as someone who earned only disgust and disrespect, including humiliation; *Dalits* were despised by the vast majority of the population. *Dalits* had no place whatsoever in Indian society.

On his final return to India, Ambedkar worked in the public service of Baroda. However, he felt forced to resign due to ill–treatment meted out to him by his colleagues.

For a period, he turned to practicing law, as well as teaching. He soon established himself as a leader of the *Dalits*. On their behalf, he published several journals. Now a *Dalit* torchbearer, he persuaded the government to accept *Dalit* representation. This huge step forward was achieved against widespread opposition, especially by certain religious groups. Ambedkar took issue with Mahatma Gandhi's political attitude to *Dalits*. In 1945, he published a comprehensive, critical article called 'What Congress and Gandhi Have Done to the Untouchables'.

In 1947, Ambedkar was appointed by the government of India as minister of justice. Among other achievements, Ambedkar took a leading role in the framing of the Indian Constitution. This outlawed Untouchability, as well as discrimination against *Dalits*. Ambedkar used all his impressive negotiating skills to steer the document through Indian political bodies until the Constitution became law on 26 January 1950. This day is now celebrated as Republic Day.

In the following year, Ambedkar resigned from the government, disappointed at his steadily diminishing influence. Subsequently, in 1956, he renounced his allegiance to Hinduism, due to the continued adoption by Hindus of Untouchability. He later became a Buddhist.

Ambedkar died on 6 December 1956, in New Delhi.

Ambendkar was a shining beacon of light. He made the impossible, possible. His achievements were, by any standard, tremendous. And he gave hope to millions, many of whom today still suffer in the dark world of *Dalits*. Throughout the history of our world, there have been a number of really great women and men. Ambedkar has joined this absolute elite group.

It is always a pleasure to end a story on a high note. Unfortunately, with respect to the *Dalits* this would be premature. It may, however, lighten our hearts a little if we briefly acknowledge progress which has been made concerning the *Dalits*.

During the last twenty-five years, two Presidents of India who were elected were *Dalits*. Nowadays, *Dalits* participate at high levels in the government. This is also the case in India's judiciary. Throughout the commercial sector, *Dalits* are often found in senior managerial positions. Simply as an indicator, of the 160 or so billionaires in India, at least 50 are *Dalit*.

None of these accomplishments masks the reality. As I have already written, in regards to *Dalits*, some progress has been made. But much remains to be done. As the saying goes – Hope Springs Eternal!

STORIES OF EUROPE

SEVEN

WARS – LIVING IN THE WORLD OF SUFFERING CIVILIANS – A CRY FROM THE HEART

On the night of 10th July 1944, a thirteen–year–old boy of Dulwich College in south London was sleeping peacefully in one of the school's boarding houses. He was suddenly awoken by a woman's firm voice.

"Wake up, Colin," she said, "get dressed and go downstairs; wait by the front door. Now!" At Dulwich, one of the first rules to be learnt was to obey authority. A little confused, I got up and dressed. By the time I was downstairs, I was getting some idea of what was happening. With the droning of aero engines, explosions in the distance and the deafeningly loud staccato bangs of Bofors anti–aircraft guns which seemed to be firing into the heavens from the road outside, little imagination was needed to realize what was happening. Another of Hitler's air raids was in progress. Only this time, there was an important difference. The aircraft which were attacking London were pilotless. The flying bomb, the V1, had arrived on the scene.

The group of about 30 boys was instructed to run from the boarding house to the first of three tuition blocks, which were linked by what were loosely called 'the cloisters'. On arrival, they would bed down in a vast cellar. As they left the house, an ear–splitting salvo from the Bofors roared over their heads.

Semi–petrified, I did my best to keep up with the running boys, most of whom were older, bigger and stronger. But my best was not good enough. Halfway to the destination, as the group ran across a large, gravelled area, I felt an elbow; then I slipped and fell. Suddenly, I was prone, alone in the sea of gravel. Now I tried to take in my new situation. I could just make out the silhouette of the science block. Apart from this, all was darkness.

The noise around me in the blackness was tremendous. Apart from the Bofors and the aero engines, there were thunderous explosions. As I got up to head for the first block, I heard the roar of an aero engine. It seemed to be flying straight at the college. I tried to run faster. Now I could see the outline of the block. Just then, the engine roar stopped. I raced to the cellar entrance. At that very moment, I heard a whine which, within a few seconds, became an intensely loud swishing, almost screaming, sound.

Then it happened. As I closed the cellar door behind me, the V1 struck the corner of the science block. The side and corner of the building I had made out, silhouetted in the darkness, were no more. The cellar, already dimly illuminated, was instantly plunged into darkness. At the same time, what had been dank air was replaced by dense, choking dust. Next to me, a voice said, "Open the door, boy." I obeyed and groped my way outside. A tall boy asked, "What is your name?"

"My name is Everard, Colin Everard." I sensed I was talking to a prefect. Then the prefect said, "You got to the cellar late. You got yourself inside just in time, didn't you? You just had a close call. Next time, don't be late. It could be too late!"

A few days later, I was attending a cricket practice. Again, we heard the engine of the V1 Doodlebug cut out. We threw ourselves on the ground and pressed our hands over our heads; and we felt our hearts pounding. After the terrifying swishing sound, there was a thunderous explosion. I heard a thud next to my head. It was a jagged piece of shrapnel. Before getting up, I touched it, which was not intelligent. I burned the tips of two fingers.

About a week later, as I left a French period, a note was handed to me. I should go back to my boarding house to see the housemaster, Eric Parsley. He was waiting for me. "Ah, Colin, you are just in time," he said. "Your father said he and your mother have had a spot of bother. That could be an English understatement." The phone rang; it was my father. "Hello, Colin. I just wanted to keep you up to date. A Doodlebug fell in our garden in the night. The whole corner was flattened. Your mother and I are all right. When we next see one another, I will tell you more. But there is not much point in you coming home for the weekend. It's best if you stay at school."

"Oh," I replied, "so you don't want me to come?" My father showed understanding to a son who apparently had little understanding. "Well, you see, Colin, we don't have a house anymore. Thank goodness you weren't in your bed at home because, with the blast, your bed was sucked out of the window. Now your bed is lying in what was our garden, on top of our uprooted plum tree."

After my parents had partially recovered from their traumatic war experience, my father related that he and his wife had been sleeping peacefully. They had suddenly been awoken by the enormous explosion. This was instantly followed by the descent of their bed; the descent stopped when their bed briefly came to rest on the dining table in the room below their bedroom.

At this point, my father dragged my mother off the table and sought protection underneath the table. Both felt they would choke with the swirling dust. A moment later, the rest of the

War causes not only physical destruction, but also death and misery to millions of innocent human beings.

house collapsed above them. Now the dust was thick, with little oxygen left around them.

After about half an hour, my father heard voices: "Everard, Everard!" My father shouted back with his choking voice – there was no audible response. Then he again heard the voices, "They must be dead – no one could survive that!" The wardens apparently then left; all was silent.

Using his back to straining point, with great difficulty, my father pushed the surrounding rubble away and gradually freed himself; eventually, he found two wardens. They then rescued my mother; this proved to be a delicate operation. Fearing that the rubble above would be disturbed, my mother's silk nightdress was cut alongside the rubble. Both freed, my parents were transported to a hospital.

During WW2, as a girl, my future wife attended nine schools. All of these changes were caused by bombing. As for myself, I was evacuated to the countryside from the 'Blitz' of London. I had no proper parental care for over two years. At one point, living in a refugee home for children, at nights I suffered traumatic nightmares.

The V1 flying bomb was superseded by the V2 rocket, a missile altogether much more powerful, and therefore destructive, than its predecessor. At Dulwich College, sitting in an English period one day, we heard a horrendous, reverberating thud. And an instant later, after some noisy juddering of the high, nineteenth-century wooden, window frames, the windows' glass shattered. Helpless, we watched fragmented glass sailing through the classroom; as the glass struck an object, it exploded into countless fragments.

Then all was quiet – and the cowering pupils continued their class work as the chill, winter air swirled around them. By now, we were used to the horrors of war; they so often seemed to be sudden and unpredictable. The only constant in the picture of war which accompanied our daily lives was destruction, both material and spiritual.

I have related these events for a primary reason: *this is the nature, the reality, of living in a war.*

When one of the recent wars began, a student friend of mine turned to me one morning and said: 'Did you hear the news? I thought we had grown out of wars.' The student could be forgiven. Europe has been largely free of wars since 1945, one of the longest periods in its war–torn history.

Yet, the numbers killed in wars in Europe is chilling. When we think of a young person whom we may have lost through illness, or perhaps killed in an accident, we are deeply saddened.

When we find that in WW1 and WW2, some 25 million military personnel lost their lives, we are numbed by the horrors of war. And in these two wars there were about 80 million civilians who lost their lives. And, of those who survived, countless numbers will suffer psychologically for the rest of their lives.

This is war!

One could go on with this litany of absolute horror and absolute sadness. On all days and nights, the news we hear, or watch on our TV screens, is full of scenes of wars. And little imagination is needed for us to dwell on death, wounded human beings, and the sheer misery inflicted on civil populations of many countries; especially, those who are poor suffer terribly in many ways. And what role do you and I play in this wretched scene? Most of us are helpless in terms of relieving this misery and pain.

What is so terribly wrong with our civilization?

Dear Reader, I ask you to really think about the horrors of wars; I also ask you to read the list of wars of the twentieth century, in which Europe has been involved. The list is shown at the end of this very short story. And I would like all of us to meditate on this terrible blot on our civilization.

It goes without saying that anything that any of us can contribute to peace, however small, is making a worthy contribution to our world community.

The following list of wars is provided by Google.

EUROPE – A LIST OF WARS OF THE TWENTIETH CENTURY

20th century

- 1903 Ilinden–Preobrazhenie Uprising
- 1904–1908 Macedonian Struggle

- 1904–1905 Russo–Japanese War
- 1905 Łódź insurrection
- 1905 Revolution of 1905
- 1906–1908 Theriso revolt
- 1907 1907 Romanian Peasants' Revolt
- 1910 Albanian Revolt of 1910
- 1910 5 October 1910 revolution
- 1911 Albanian Revolt of 1911
- 1911–1912 Italo–Turkish War
- 1912 Albanian Revolt of 1912
- 1912–1913 Balkan Wars
    - 1912–1913 First Balkan War
    - 1913 Tikveš Uprising
    - 1913 Second Balkan War
- 1913 Ohrid–Debar Uprising
- 1914 Peasant Revolt in Albania
- 1914–1918 World War I – 19,174,335 deaths
    - 1914 Caucasus Campaign
    - 1916 Noemvriana
    - 1917 Toplica Uprising
    - 1918 Judenburg mutiny
    - 1918 Cattaro Mutiny
    - 1918 Aster Revolution
    - 1918 Radomir Rebellion
    - 1918 Finnish Civil War
- 1916 Easter Rising
- 1917 Russian Revolution
    - 1917 February Revolution
    - 1917 July Days
    - 1917 Polubotkivtsi uprising
    - 1917 Kornilov affair

- 1917 October Revolution
    - 1917 Junker mutiny
- 1917 Kerensky–Krasnov uprising
- 1917–1921 Russian Civil War
- 1917–1918 Red Army invasion of Georgia
- 1917–1921 Ukrainian War of Independence
    - 1917–1921 Ukrainian–Soviet War
    - 1918–1919 Polish–Ukrainian War
- 1918–1924 Left–wing uprisings against the Bolsheviks
    - 1918 Left SR uprising
    - 1921 Kronstadt rebellion
- 1918–1922 Heimosodat
    - 1918 Vienna expedition
    - 1918 Aunus expedition
    - 1918–1920 Petsamo expeditions
    - 1918–1920 National revolt of Ingrian Finns
    - 1921–1922 East Karelian Uprising
- 1918–1920 Estonian War of Independence
- 1918–1925 Allied intervention in the Russian Civil War
    - 1918–1920 North Russia Intervention
    - 1918–1922 Siberian Intervention
- 1918 Georgian–Armenian War
- 1918–1920 Georgian–Ossetian conflict (1918–20)
- 1918–1919 Georgian–Russian conflict over Sochi
- 1918–1920 Armenian–Azerbaijani War
- 1918–1920 Latvian War of Independence
- 1918–1920 Lithuanian Wars of Independence
    - 1918–1919 Lithuanian–Soviet War
    - 1919 Lithuanian War of Independence (War against the Bermontians)
    - 1920 Polish–Lithuanian War

    - 1919–1921 Polish–Soviet War
    - 1921 Georgian–Russian War
    - 1924 Georgian Uprising against Soviet Union
- 1919–1920 Revolutions and interventions in Hungary (1918–20)
    - 1918–1919 Hungarian–Romanian War
    - 1918–1919 Hungarian–Czechoslovak War
- 1919 Sejny Uprising
- 1919 Khotyn Uprising
- 1918–1919 Austro–Slovene conflict in Carinthia
- 1918–1958 Polish–Czechoslovak border conflicts
- 1919 Polish–Czech war for Teschen Silesia
- 1918–1919 German Revolution
- 1918–1919 Greater Poland Uprising
- 1919–1922 Greco–Turkish War
- 1918–1921 Franco–Turkish War
- 1920 Armenian–Turkish War
- 1919 Christmas Uprising
- 1919–1920 Unrest in Split
- 1919–1921 Silesian Uprisings
    - 1919 First Silesian Uprising
    - 1920 Second Silesian Uprising
    - 1921 Third Silesian Uprising
- 1919–1922 Irish War of Independence
- 1920 Husino rebellion
- 1920 Vlora War
- 1920 Kapp Putsch
- 1920 Ruhr Uprising
- 1920 Slutsk Defence Action
- 1920–1924 Biennio Rosso
- 1921 Uprising in West Hungary
- 1921 February Uprising

- 1921 Charles IV of Hungary's attempts to retake the throne
- 1922–1923 Irish Civil War
- 1923 Corfu incident
- 1923 September Uprising
- 1923 Klaipèda Revolt
- 1923 Leonardopoulos–Gargalidis coup d'état attempt
- 1924 1924 Estonian coup d'état attempt
- 1924 August Uprising
- 1925 Incident at Petrich
- 1932 Mäntsälä rebellion
- 1933 Casas Viejas incident
- 1933 Anarchist uprising in Spain (1933)
- 1934 Asturian miners' strike of 1934
- 1934 Austrian Civil War
- 1935 1935 Greek coup d'état attempt
- 1936–1939 Spanish Civil War
- 1938 1938 Greek coup d'état attempt
- 1939 German occupation of Czechoslovakia
- 1939 Hungarian invasion of Carpatho–Ukraine
- 1939 Italian invasion of Albania
- 1939–1965 Spanish Maquis
- 1939–1940 S–Plan
- 1939–1945 World War II
    - 1939 Nazi German invasion of Poland
    - 1939 Soviet invasion of Poland
    - 1939–1940 Winter War (Soviet invasion of Finland)
    - 1940 Phoney War
    - 1940 Operation Weserübung
    - 1940 Norwegian campaign
    - 1940 Invasion of Luxembourg
    - 1940 Battle of the Netherlands

    - 1940 Battle of Belgium
    - 1940 Battle of France
    - 1940 Italian invasion of France
    - 1940 Soviet invasion of the Baltic States
    - 1940 Soviet occupation of Bessarabia and Northern Bukovina
    - 1940 Battle of Britain
    - 1940–1941 Greco–Italian War
    - 1941–1945 Soviet–German War
    - 1941–1945 Yugoslav anti–fascist resistance movement
    - 1941–1944 Continuation War
    - 1941 Uprising in Montenegro
    - 1942 Case Blue
    - 1942–1944 Northern Campaign
    - 1942–1956 Ukrainian Insurgent Army
    - 1943 Italian Campaign
    - 1944 Operation Market Garden
    - 1944 Warsaw Uprising
    - 1944 Western Allied invasion of Germany
    - 1944–1945 Lapland War
    - 1944–1945 Slovak National Uprising
    - 1944–1945 Liberation of France
    - 1944–1945 Battle of the Bulge
    - 1945 Second Battle of the Alps
    - 1945 Battle of Berlin
- 1944–1956 Guerrilla war in the Baltic states
- 1945–1949 Greek Civil War
- 1946–1948 Corfu Channel incident
- 1947–1962 Romanian anti–communist resistance movement
- 1953 Uprising in East Germany
- 1955–1959 Cyprus Emergency
- 1956 Uprising in Poznań

- 1956 Hungarian Revolution
- 1956–1962 Operation Harvest
- 1958 First Cod War
- 1959–2011 Basque conflict
- 1967 Greek coup d'état
- 1968 Warsaw Pact invasion of Czechoslovakia
- 1968–1998 The Troubles
- 1970–1984 Unrest in Italy
- 1972–1973 Second Cod War
- 1974 Turkish invasion of Cyprus
- 1974 Carnation Revolution
- 1975 Coup of 25 November 1975
- 1975–1976 Third Cod War
- 1976–2016 Corsican conflict
- 1981 Spanish coup d'état attempt
- 1986 Evros River incident
- 1988–1994 First Nagorno–Karabakh War
- 1989–1995 Gagauzia conflict
- 1989 Romanian Revolution
- 1990 Log Revolution
- 1990–1991 Soviet attacks on Lithuanian border posts
- 1990–present Transnistria conflict
    - 1990–1992 Transnistria War
- 1991 January Events
- 1991 The Barricades
- 1991–2001 Yugoslav Wars
    - 1991 Ten–Day War
    - 1991–1995 Croatian War of Independence
    - 1992–1995 Bosnian War
    - 1992–1994 Croat–Bosniak War
    - 1995–1998 Insurgency in Kosovo

    - 1998–1999 Kosovo War
    - 1999–2001 Insurgency in the Preševo Valley
    - 2001 2001 insurgency in Macedonia
- 1991–1992 Georgian war against Russo–Ossetian alliance
- 1991–1993 Georgian Civil War
- 1991–2017 Chechen–Russian conflict
    - 1994 Battle of Grozny (November 1994)
    - 1994–1996 First Chechen War

EIGHT

A WORLD OF SURPRISES – THE PARTY

Some years ago, I worked in Eastern Africa, in the East African Community. With my qualification and experience in the fields of logistics, I was appointed (with the approval of the presidents of Kenya, Uganda and Tanzania) as East Africa's first chief supplies officer. Just when I was installing myself in my new job, I received a phone call that the secretary general of the E. A. Community wished to see me.

Sitting in Dunstan Omari's office, Dunstan Omari explained that the three–countries' organization was facing a problem. The E.A. Community had been trying to conclude a Treaty of Association with the European Economic Communities (the EEC was the forerunner of the EU); however, the negotiations had failed. Despite requests by the E.A. Community for further meetings, the Europeans showed disinterest.

Dunstan Omari then explained that the East Africans now wanted to convince the Europeans that they meant business; to this end, the East Africans would establish a mission in Brussels to liaise with the EEC. He then said that if I were asked to establish an office for the pygmies in Rwanda or Burundi, I would have a problem trying to do so. The East Africans were now faced with a similar problem – they would have little confidence working in Europe.

Dunstan Omari then said that, after several consultations, the consensus was that I should represent the East Africans vis–à–vis the European EEC and that, without delay, I should travel to Brussels to establish the E.A. Mission.

Over a period of the following three months, I completed my assigned task.

On arrival in Brussels in late Autumn, I installed myself in the residential Park Hotel, close to the EEC buildings. Monsieur Robert was usually at the reception; he was a lean, dark–haired man in his forties and always wore a light grey jacket. As I was either on my way out of the hotel or returning, we often exchanged a few words.

My work routine was demanding. I was up at 6a.m. to write an account of the previous day's activities; the report then had to be telexed to Nairobi. Then, after a quick breakfast, I was 'doing the rounds'. Suitable premises had to be found for the East African Mission; the premises needed to be furnished, staff had to be found and given employment contracts, the office car had to be bought and so forth. Naturally, I had to deal at length with the city authorities. Apart from having to execute many daily tasks myself (this was a one–man operation), just one factor (of several) which was a disadvantage for me was that most 'commercial' individuals preferred to meet in the evening, and several negotiations extended past midnight. So, I had to get used to a sleep of four or five hours at night.

Towards the end of my assignment, a quite large delegation from East Africa arrived in Brussels. This included the three ministers of economic affairs from Kenya, Tanzania and Uganda; they were supported by the usual entourage of officials. In terms of knowledge, his personality and natural leadership qualities, Mwai Kibaki of Kenya, who was recognized as a brilliant economist, stood head and shoulders above everyone else. As a short, interesting digression, I should record that Mwai Kibaki was born of a Kikuyu family in the Highlands of Kenya. As a baby, he slept on the mud floor of a typical tribal, very small house, which resembled a hut, constructed of mud and wattle. After a truly brilliant career, he ended his life as President of Kenya, living in the palatial President's Residence.

The officials struck me as a motley bunch. Some looked professionally earnest, but others behaved as though they were on a sight seeing tour. A few were loud and somewhat arrogant (usually a sign of insecurity and lack of confidence). In any case, one early evening, a small group announced that they would later be visiting a night club – "Striptease, striptease, Colin." They were keen that I should accompany them. I thanked them; however, I explained that I had been working flat–out for weeks – all I wanted to do was to snatch some rest. I told them my presence would be unrewarding; I begged to be excused.

Mwai Kibaki. As a child, he lived in a tribal house, with a mud floor - He ended his life living as President of Kenya, in a palatial residence.

The officials would have none of it, and they pressed me so strongly that I eventually agreed. But I warned them that I was hopelessly tired. In the evening, we entered the night club. There was a bar, tables and a small vacant area, which I presumed was for dancing. I did my best. I tried to be jovial and happy. But for me, there was no escape: After perhaps an hour, I fell asleep.

Then I was awoken by the noise of loud clapping. On the little dance floor was a somewhat short, plump girl; she was naked and one of her hands twirled her underpants. Totally disinterested, I fell asleep again. But suddenly, I was awake; there was a tapping on my shoulder. I slowly opened my eyes; apparently, I was looking at the club's proprietor. He simply said, "You are bad for my business. Please leave!" With relief, I left. As I slowly walked to the Park Hotel, I had the feeling I was sleepwalking.

Shortly after his arrival, Mr. Kibaki took me to one side and explained that, after recent exchanges, both the Europeans and East Africans were now motivated to reach an agreement on a Treaty of Association. He seemed to take a liking to me and expressed admiration on what, single–handedly, I had achieved; in addition to establishing the mission, I had called on senior EEC officials, expressing the hope that fruitful results would follow the establishment of the mission. After further discussion, Mr. Kibaki said it would be appropriate for me to be included in the delegation; from the morrow, I should sit with the East Africans, behind Mr. Kibaki, in the large meeting room. After three more days of negotiations, it was clear that the basis existed for agreement on the Treaty.

On the conclusion of the fifth day of discussions, as we left the meeting room, Mr. Kibaki turned and took my arm. We sat in a little side room, where the minister said, "Mr. Everard, I want to thank you for all you are doing to strengthen the hand of the East Africans. As you know, we are now well on the way to agreeing to the draft of the treaty. So, I think we should have a celebration. We should have a cocktail party in the premises of the new East African Mission. I will organise the invitations; there will be about fifty. We can have the party one week today at 6.30p.m. I know it is not your job, but will you please organise the party – thank you!"

That day, on my return to the Park Hotel, I discussed with M. Robert all the requirements for the party. M. Robert was enthusiastic. Yes, the hotel could and would provide absolutely everything for the party, including the waiters. We listed the canapés (snacks), champagne, plates, dishes, glasses, cutlery and so forth. It was agreed that everything which had been listed and signed for by me would be ready on the appointed day at 4p.m., to be transported to the new mission, which was about three kilometres distant.

A week later, I slipped out of the meeting room early and walked briskly through the park to the hotel. There, as usual, stood Mr. Robert. I was in a confident, jovial mood. "Well, M. Robert, here we are," I said. "I am sure all is ready? We can start loading the cars, don't you think?" In response, I received a routine, somewhat blank, "Hello, Mr. Everard." I repeated my question; this time M. Robert looked uncomfortable. Then he said, "I am sorry. I have completely forgotten about your party! We have nothing."

My immediate reaction was to strike the reception counter. M. Robert's face paled, and he seemed to stoop, hoping to take cover! "Well, M. Robert," I said firmly, "you and the hotel staff are going to have to move and get organized very, very fast!" Although the staff's movements seemed quite disorganized, in fact, things began to happen quite quickly. One of the waiters, who repeatedly addressed me as 'Son Excellence!', soon found other waiters and was effective in co-ordinating the whole operation.

About an hour or so later, I was sitting with the chauffeur of the BMW and two waiters, laden with food, champagne and so forth, en route to the mission. But now it was the rush hour; so, after 45 minutes of edging our way around the hotel block, we had reached only a point directly behind the hotel.

At last, we reached the mission. Our arrival coincided with another; this was a black Mercedes 600. As an ambassador got out of the car, I nimbly hopped through the front garden, reaching the front door just in time to welcome the ambassador with a warm handshake and a smile.

During the next twenty minutes or so, all the guests arrived and, to my surprise, things were functioning well. There was, of course, some delay before the champagne was properly chilled; but no one seemed to mind. In fact, after about an hour, it became obvious that the champagne was being consumed more quickly than we had estimated. So, I went outside to ask the chauffeur to return to the hotel and bring more cases of champagne. Although I had told the chauffeur that he was to stay in the car, he was nowhere to be seen. So, I began to search the mission premises. Soon, on the first floor, I found the chauffeur. He was holding the newly recruited economics assistant (formerly of the OECD) in his arms. I reminded the chauffeur that his duty was to stay in the car. "Chauffeur," exclaimed the assistant, "he told me he was a film star!"

Although the party was supposed to be a six-to-eight affair, it was now almost nine o'clock. And not a single guest showed any sign of leaving. How long would they stay? And what about the supply of food and drink? The happy chit chat went from crescendo to yet another. Now the Tanzania minister approached me. Sheikh Babu said above the noise, "Mr. Everard, what a wonderful party. But where is the photographer?"

"Your Excellency," I responded, "I thought one would need a photographer in the meeting room at the time the draft treaty will be agreed. But I thought not at a party." Sheikh Babu was a big man; he was reputed to have blood on his hands in Zanzibar. He gave me a quick, stern look. "I demand you to have a photographer here within twenty minutes." Then he left me.

I called the Hotel Metropole and fifteen minutes later, the photographer was busy taking innumerable photos. After another fifteen minutes, with myself thinking that the zealous photographer was showing excessive enthusiasm, I suggested to him that he had taken more than an adequate number of photos. If he would kindly give me the address of his *atelier*, I would perhaps pass by in a couple of days and purchase some selected photos.

The demeanor of the man changed instantly. Instead of the happy fellow who had been smiling as he nimbly passed from one guest to the next to snap his camera, now I was confronted with a scowling face and a body taut with angry nerves. "What are you talking about – selected photos?" he asked.

"Well," I responded, "of course, ideally it would be nice to buy all the photos you have taken, but as you know, in practice, this is rarely the case. So, I will purchase the better photos."

His response was quick and decisive! With fury in his eyes and trembling lips, the photographer blurted out, "So you think you can play with me – you are a filthy Englishman! You will *never* get a single photo from me."

The photographer quickly gathered his things and strode to the entrance of the mission. He pulled the inner door open, went through and slammed the door behind him with such force that the glazed upper half of the door shattered with a loud crash – and countless glass fragments flew through the air of the hallway.

Suddenly, the ever–louder voices of the guests were hushed. But, after a few seconds, their curiosity apparently satisfied, the party continued. “Son Excellence!” I heard. It was the self–appointed head waiter. I should not worry; the glass fragments would be cleared up immediately.

The party came to what one might say its natural end; it was a little after 10p.m. By ‘natural’, I mean the guests had had more than their fill of food and drink. So, it was time to go home. As I shook hands with the last departing guest, I noticed a large Mercedes in the road outside. The rear door was open. Then I saw that the guest’s well–attired body was partly lying on the back seat; so far, so good. But what about the legs? Motionless, they were hanging over the end of the bench seat, apparently unable to follow the body. I lifted the legs, pushed them into the car and asked the chauffeur to do his best to see the occupant safely home.

Shortly before eleven o’clock, I felt it was high time to lock up the premises and return to the Park Hotel. Before doing so, I would check that all was in order. Starting on the third floor, I suddenly heard hushed voices. Yes, again, there was the economics assistant in the arms of the chauffeur. I asked them to give themselves a break and to give me a hand in clearing up a few things. Then I locked up the premises.

Two days later, I made an appointment with the photographer. In his *atelier,* all the photos were neatly arranged. After I had selected some good photos which I thought should please the ministers, I bought them. The photographer was again his pleasant self. As I thanked him, shook his hand and said goodbye, he hugged me, kissed me on both cheeks and described me as a charming Englishman!

A few days later, the ministers and their officials returned to East Africa. As far as I was concerned, I would see the mission operating effectively – and at last I would enjoy some sleep. I scheduled my departure two weeks later, by which time the chief of mission would have arrived.

With time on my hands, I decided to explore the possibility of playing some golf. Soon I was at the delightful Tervuren Golf Club. This was a typicalm very goodm inland course – so well kept and so green! The clubhouse was a converted chateau.

One day, having hired a bag of clubs and paid my green fee, I approached the first tee, to drive off. Standing on the tee was a good–looking young woman. As is normal, I introduced myself and suggested that we might play together (under golf etiquette, singletons have no standing on a golf course). The woman seemed to look me up and down; then she said, "No, thank you." She then hit a beautiful drive up the middle of the lush fairway. When the golfer was out of range, I also hit off.

At the halfway point, that was, having played nine holes, I stood under a shady tree, motionless in accordance with golf etiquette. I was waiting for the woman to drive off the tenth tee. But instead of hitting the ball, the woman dropped her club on the grass and walked towards me. "What are you doing, standing under the tree?" she asked. "Well,' I replied, 'I am keeping my distance to make sure I don't disturb your concentration."

Without another word, this good–looking young woman smiled, took my arm and said, "I have been watching you. You know how to hit a golf ball. We can play together."

When I play tournament golf, I never talk to anyone; I am concentrating. And so it was that day. I played those nine holes just one shot above par, the professional standard. But the woman won – by one stroke.

Before parting company with her, I congratulated this fine golfer on her win. I hoped perhaps one day I would be given the chance for revenge. Then she said, "Yes, you played well, but, of course, you were up against it – just now, I am the Belgian Ladies Champion. Colin, I enjoyed playing with you. For once, I had some competition. Adieu!"

On my return to Nairobi, I took up my new position as chief supplies officer for the three countries of the East African Community, Kenya, Tanzania and Uganda.

With my wife and my children, we enjoyed living in Nairobi. We rented a pleasant single–story stone house, which had a large garden; the drive up to the house was a hundred metres in length. One day, we were doing a little shopping in the nearby shopping centre. As I was selecting some white carnations for my wife, suddenly, a strong voice rang out. I turned and was face to face with Mwai Kibaki; he was beaming. Smiling, he embraced me. Then I introduced the minister to my wife, Emy.

"Mr. Everard," he said, "what a great pleasure to see you again. I will always remember you from when we were in Brussels together. You know, both the Europeans and the East African countries recently ratified the Treaty of Association and the treaty was fully signed. But I must tell you one thing. For me in Brussels, there was one event that I will *never* forget – the party!"

NINE

ANOTHER WORLD – SKIING IN HEAVEN

Dear Reader, have you visited heaven? I have – or now, I wonder, have I? I was convinced I was in heaven; and I was not dreaming. Yes, can you imagine, I was skiing there! Let me tell you about my visit to heaven. Then you can make your own judgement.

A few years ago, I found myself in the winter in Austria. One day, I booked rooms in a little hotel in a township in central Austria; the township is called Kaprun. Kaprun is situated south of Salzburg, a city famous internationally for its wonderful music festival and for one of Austria's foremost composers, Wolfgang Amadeus Mozart.

The drive from Vienna to Kaprun was nothing less than a sheer delight. Much of the scenery was beautiful, especially the magnificent landscape of huge mountains, south of Salzburg. As we neared Kaprun, we looked skywards; there, with the snow and glaciers glistening in the bright sunlight, we could see the snow–capped Kitzsteinhorn. This huge mountain towers to 3,200 meters (about 10,500 feet) above sea level. In the lower reaches of the mountain, the trees were clothed in a hoar frost. The incredibly beautiful trees looked almost unreal in the snow; they stood out in what seemed like a vast white carpet. The scene before our eyes was simply gorgeous in the bright sunshine.

Kaprun lies 750 meters above sea level. In winter, it is a typical winter–sports center. In Kaprun, if you walk about in the early evening after some skiing, you pass one or two hotels and a few inviting cafes; so, there is no problem in finding some strengthening refreshment. If you feel like dancing, the odd discothèque is not far away. Kaprun is a happy place, without being noisy. Also, some nice shops help to create an atmosphere of permanence and prosperity. The owner of a lovely jewelry shop told me that there are plenty of shoppers from eastern Europe, including a good number of Oligarchs; in summer, wealthy Arabs, usually accompanied by entourages, stay for a few months in Kaprun, happy to escape their summer heat.

Not that Kaprun needs to worry too much about its survival. It was first mentioned as a settlement in 950A.D. Even its formidable castle, which was built above the little town about 650 years ago, has been fully restored during the last thirty years. Kaprun is one of those places where you always seem to feel well. And when you are plodding around in the snow, one enjoys the picturesque silhouettes of, for example, the overhanging roofs of the houses, not to mention the brightly lit, elegant window displays of the shops. You can easily think how these lovely surroundings contribute to a feeling of well–being.

On arrival at the hotel, all the skis (two pairs each for downhill, three others for cross–country skiing) were placed in a temperature–controlled storage room; here, we also noticed heated horizontal bars where one could place ski boots, to be kept warm. After a hearty dinner, we were happy to see that our bedrooms each had a large balcony, and each room had a view over the rooftops, directly to the Kitzsteinhorn massif and adjacent mountains.

Next morning, I awoke at about 7 and opened the door to

the balcony. This was my first glimpse of heaven! Although the sun was not yet up, the sky had become a sheet of gold. The whole scene of the range of mountains was nothing less than a panorama of beauty; I was incredulous, almost mesmerised. Half an hour later, the rays of the rising sun began to illuminate the vast snowfields of the mountains.

Soon we were ready for some cross–country skiing. As we left the hotel, I asked where we should start; the starting point was five minutes away. As we carried our skis to the start, I thought to myself, 'Now, take it easy, you haven't been on skis for a while; although you feel you can't wait, don't rush!'

Now for some action! Everything went well. The trails around Kaprun were well–groomed and the temperature was perfect for cross–country skiing. The lovely trails near Kaprun are in fact part of a network of some 250 kilometers of trails. On the first morning, we skied six kilometers or so in the morning.

Over the following few days, we skied for several hours. But however far we thought we had skied, we were happy to know there were many more kilometres left for us; in fact, probably more than 200 kilometres! In any case, whether in the open, traversing the vast expanse of virgin white, or gliding through woodland, the spirit was uplifted by the sheer beauty of the surroundings. How often does one have the privilege of enjoying nature clothed in the indescribable beauty of limitless snow, with billions of ice crystals which glitter like diamonds as they are touched by the sun's rays? At every turn, we encountered indescribable beauty. Yes, we were privileged indeed!

Andrea is the youngest of our four daughters. Andrea is the finest, and most elegant, skier one might find. So, we always skied together. I usually simply followed Andrea with complete confidence.

The Kitzsteinhorn in central Austria

With our muscles somewhat strengthened, we decided it was time to start the alpine skiing. We bought a pass for the rest of the week: The pass entitled us to use any of the ski lifts in the area; these numbered 60, with the pistes (runs) offering 130 kilometres of alpine skiing. At the start of the ski runs, each run showed the level of difficulty. Most of the time, we chose intermediate-level runs, occasionally the most difficult. I knew that Andrea would have little problem in navigating difficult stretches; I also knew that so long as I would simply follow her, we would jointly manage to enjoy our skiing successfully. On this first occasion, I was pleased with my so-called carving skis; they functioned well with me.

The weather in Kaprun remained concisely fine for the week. There was, however, a weather element which was described as an inversion; this meant that it was significantly colder in the valleys than on top of the mountains. For example, one morning, we had a temperature outside the hotel of –16C. At the same time, high up at the Alpine Centre on the Kitzsteinhorn (almost

2,500 metres above sea level) the temperature was –4C degrees, some 12C warmer. This pattern persisted for the whole week.

Now it was time to tackle higher mountains. The gondola took us up to 1,545 metres (5,100 feet); from the top gondola station, one could continue with other lifts to almost 1,700 metres. The following day, we took a lift up a mountain which rises from the edge of a nearby lake. At the top of the mountain, it was 2,000 metres (6,600 feet) a.s.l. As for my skiing, this delightful visit to the mountains around Kaprun helped me to graduate to Intermediate/Parallel skier.

The skiing in the mountains was sometimes challenging; some of the pitches were quite long and steep. We progressed downwards steadily and well. Not once did I feel that I might fall, even on the steepest sections or when sometimes the snow surface was slightly thin, even icy. Andrea mentioned that our skis were new, and the edges were sharp; so, this must have made a positive difference.

Our evenings were great fun and sometimes hilarious. Once, for example, we had returned to the hotel in the late afternoon and explored possibilities for some refreshment in the center of the little town. Usually, we asked for hot red wine or hunter tea – this is strong tea with rum. These drinks stimulate not only warmth, but also good cheer!

One afternoon, we walked further up the prettily lit street until we found a shop which not only had a wonderful choice of breads and cakes, but also served coffee and tea. We sat at a table in the corner and asked for two hunter teas. Shortly after, very hot drink was brought in by a good–looking woman; hot steam swirled around handsome, light brown mugs. The woman, who chatted delightfully, was the shop's owner. The lively woman continued talking while we waited a few minutes for the delicious drink to cool a little. We reached for our mugs.

Then it happened! As I reached for my mug with happy anticipation, suddenly Andrea looked at me with alarm, eyes widening by the split second. Then I took a sip; my throat was attacked by the sheer force of the drink and my lips had lost feeling – the instant impact of the drink was dynamite! I tried to speak – but this proved to be impossible. Any case, my mouth was on fire. The only sound I could make was a slightly high–pitched 'U–u–gh!'. Andrea was already laughing. I sat motionless, limp in my chair, from time to time I was wondering when I might be able to speak again. Then we heard the sweet voice of the daughter of the house; she was working behind the counter: "Maybe you put a bit too much rum in the hunter teas, Mother?" Perhaps that was a monumental understatement.

Now we were laughing; and we wondered if we would ever stop laughing. Of course, for us, this would now be the only place in Kaprun where we would ever drink hunter tea. The next day, we were back, although, this time, we asked for less rum. "Yesterday, you found it a little too strong? Very well, no problem." Yes, it was the good–looking owner, a woman of real charm. When Andrea mentioned that we would be departing for Vienna at the end of the week, she told us to be sure to return the following year; then she smiled gently, shook our hands and wished us a safe journey.

After dinner (whether it was heartily Austrian, Italian or Gala), our main pastime was to play a card game of the distant past; its name is 'tarock'. The game uses special, brightly coloured cards, of singular design. The game needs knowledge and imaginative approach. As far as the possible results are concerned, these seem limitless and often surprising. Above all, tarock is a game which favours a quick wit and perception. It also invariably encourages humour, linked with enjoyment.

Soon it would be time to visit the Kitzsteinhorn massif. The day before, we had cross–country skied. On our way back to the hotel, we passed a small ski shop. There, I met the owner, Maresa; I asked her whether she could give me an instructor for a day or two. Maresa gave me Erich; he was not only an expert skier, but also a delightfully courteous and cheerful man. Naturally, he was familiar with the many trails on the Kitzsteinhorn. Erich, an Austrian through and through, would certainly be able to give me a few tips, especially on the most challenging runs, where good technique was vital.

On the next morning, Andrea and I picked up Erich and we set off for the Glacier Jet gondola station. This was a new high–speed lift system installed by the Austrian firm of Doppelmayr. To digress briefly, the American owner of the Salt Lake Olympic Mountain area commented that he chose Dopplmayr lift systems because they are simply the best; he likened Dopplmayr to 'the Cadillac of ski lifts'.

When we arrived, there was a crush of humanity trying to board the gondola. At last, it was our turn to get into the slowly moving gondola; to board, we found ourselves competing with a bunch of English school children. They were probably on their way to a skiing class. "What a *terrible squash!* My sandwiches have been pressed together!" shouted a little fellow, with some affectation; he was obviously looking ahead to a lunch, which had already been partly spoiled. "Do you learn German at school?" I asked him. "No, everyone knows English!" he replied. "Maybe eventually we will learn some German. Now we learn Latin." I persevered, "Why not learn some languages?" The answer was not exactly rational, although it was very much to the point: "My language is English." Bless him!

The first part of the gondola route rises rapidly near deep

cliffs of bare rock, separated by rugged cleavages. There are some trees, but the deep, almost vertical rocks prevent normal tree growth. Soon the gondola swings over the top of the cliffs and the snowfields come into view. On either side are great mountains, clothed in white, towering towards the heavens.

The ride to the gondola station (2,000 metres a.s.l.) takes about fifteen minutes. Here, one transfers to the second stage of the high–speed lift; this takes one up to 2,450 metres a.s.l, where one finds the Alpine Centre. From here, there are several chair lifts and tows, which take the skier up to the higher points of the mountain; the highest elevation is then reached, that is 3,000 metres, almost 10,000 feet a.s.l.

Having arrived at the main lift's highest elevation, Erich announced we should take a lift to the highest point of the mountain, which we did. Erich took me with him on a tow; the tow is only for two, so Andrea followed us, just behind. Now we were up on a high ridge of the mountain. Looking down, one could be forgiven for being awestruck by the panorama of mountains. The scene of mountains seemed never–ending, as we scanned the incredible view which stretched into the distance. Far below us were the peaks of mountains where we had skied a day or two previously; the peaks of these were at about 1,750 metres ; yet for us, they looked like Lilliput! Then we looked upwards. We were overwhelmed by the deep azure, as the ultraviolet rays made their presence felt. The depth and density of the blue was amazing. Now we were in a different world.

A thought flashed through my senses. Was this the edge of heaven?

"Just follow me." Erich's good–natured command distracted me from my heavenly thoughts. Down we went, descending about a thousand metres. The quality of the snow was perfect for skiing. There was just enough resistance to give the skis a good, purposeful feel; at the same time, you could let the skis slide as fast as you might wish. As always, the elegant Andrea was hovering and gliding gracefully just behind me. Erich seemed to take the descent quite seriously; perhaps he was concerned about the level of my ability. At the Alpine Centre, he made the odd complimentary comment, stating that part of the descent included some slightly less than expert-level stretches; he thought I had managed well.

After another run, I mentioned to Erich that I thought his time was already past the agreed two hours for which I had paid. He smiled. "The boss is not here. I am happy with you two. We can ski as long as you like." So, we did.

The next day, Erich picked up Andrea in the morning and they went skiing for the day. He showed Andrea so many runs on the Kitzsteinhorn. I was happy for the two of them, I went cross–country skiing. The sheer beauty of the trees was breathtaking. Each one seemed to be a singularly sculptured masterpiece of ice crystals, which shimmered in the brilliant sunshine.

The next day would be our last. Chatting with Erich, he was suddenly smiling; then he said, "Tomorrow is my day off. If you like, we can ski together again. If you happen to meet Maresa and she asks about me, just say you haven't seen me!" Next day, at one-thirty, Andrea and I met Erich at the Alpine Centre. Up we went. This time, Erich explained, we would go again to one of the highest points on the Kitzsteinhorn which is served by a tow. On top it was windswept; the altitude was 3,200 metres.

Because of the weather conditions, Erich decided that we should descend. He chose the route we should use. Looking down, we could see skiers; they looked like pinheads in the snow. Then I looked at the slope; it seemed steep, I thought. "Just follow me.", Erich's usual command calmly broke through the noise of the chill wind.

Down we went. All was well – no problem. Erich turned to us. "That run is what we call deep red. That is, it is not a black, expert run, but it is on the borderline. There could have been an easier way down, but I knew you could do it, Colin, and you did it!" Then Andrea spoke: "Erich, go off and ski somewhere for an hour. Now I want to ski with my father." Erich did not seem at all taken aback; he just smiled and dutifully left us! "Don't worry about him, Daddy," Andrea explained, "he seems to know so many people on the mountain." In any case, Andrea and I had a wonderful time; we always skid so well together.

After about an hour, we met Erich at the highest station of the Glacier Jet Lift. From there, we walked through a tunnel for 350 metres. As we reached the end of the tunnel, our senses could hardly take in the panoramic view. It was breathtaking. Among the glorious mountain peaks, at centre stage rose the Grossglockner (Big Bell), the highest mountain in Austria. It has an altitude of 3,798 metres (12,500 feet) a.s.l.

The world of mountains is another world. And this other world is a heavenly place. If you want to sort out some thoughts, if you would like your soul to be uplifted and nourished, go to the mountains. There you will find heaven!

On the next morning, we left the hotel, where we had been very well looked after. Mentally, we had to prepare to re–enter the world in which we usually live. We passed the wonderful trees covered in hoar frost. And as we bade adieu, we tried to take in the enchanting beauty of the mountains. Our eyes moved naturally towards the majestic Kitzsteinhorn, which was yet again glistening in the gorgeous sunshine. Just before it passed from view, my senses were touched by a thought. 'Yes, it is heaven' – and we were there.

Dear Reader, I hope we are still progressing together.

A good number of years ago, I was skiing with another daughter. The conditions were not as pleasant as they were in the story above. In any case, I had an accident. As I was recovering, I decided to record what happened. Now I will reproduce what I wrote.

THE SKI PATROL

(or the diary of a bureaucratic skier)

I have always enjoyed physical challenge. For the desk–bound worker, skiing offers not only relaxation but as much instantaneous physical challenge as anyone could seek. It was with these thoughts in mind that, after a particularly hectic three months in the office, I decided to put it all behind me for one glorious day and ski with one of my charming daughters. Although that particular Friday was not exactly one of the more inspiring in terms of the weather, we were, however, fortunate in that it was not incredibly cold.

We chose a big mountain. As we sat in the chairlift, we occasionally caught a glimpse of blue sky as the rather low veils of cloud were blown rapidly across the wintry sun. I tend to think of a chair on a cable as a little island in space. One is out of contact with Mother Earth and, except for one's companion sitting next to one, one is remote from one's fellow human beings. For me, the chairlift is a place for thought, a seat from where, as you rise up the mountain, if you purse your lips, you can 'drink' in the wonderfully clean, crisp mountain air; and it is a pedestal from which you can indulge in sheer visual pleasure. One may look down at a sea of soft green fir trees; or, as the lift reaches a higher elevation, one may find oneself almost in awe, as the scene changes to a silvery-white wonderland. Sometimes, looking up to the azure above, the green and blue meet on a brief horizon; one may be reminded of the adage, 'Blue and green should never be seen'. When you have seen them meet on a mountain, you can have no doubt that they should.

The wind was blowing quite hard on top of the mountain, and we found that, with it blowing on our backs, we could traverse the white expanse effortlessly. I watched my daughter; she was moving like a figurine, moving gracefully in the icy conditions high up on the shoulder of the mountain. Soon we would be below the top and perhaps it would be more sheltered.

"Let's try that run over there," I tried to shout above the wind. We traversed towards the start of the run. As we were about to descend, I noticed the ski patrol helping a young girl on to a stretcher. We have all seen the ski patrol, but few of us have contact with them. Perhaps we have thought from time to time that they are undoubtedly excellent skiers; we also know they can help in an emergency, but happily this particular raison d'être does not concern most of us.

I hesitated. The first part of the descent was steep and uneven. It must be tricky, I thought, for the ski patrol to manipulate the stretcher down a section like that. We watched them for a few moments. Now it was time for us to start the descent.

I turned to my daughter. "We should not risk skiing near the ski patrol; they have their hands full with the injured girl. Instead of going straight down here, we can easily ski by the side of the main run over there, down that narrow trail through the trees; we can cut back at the bottom, and we shall be ahead of the ski patrol. Then we won't press them or distract them. Let's go."

Down we went, back and forth; descending rapidly, it was rather as though we were plunging down a huge, uneven stairway. Now and then, the skis were noisy, as they bit into and scraped the icy patches. Three–quarters of the way down that stretch, I stopped to watch my daughter a short distance above me. She was descending safely and looked elegant in her new boots. So, I went on.

Then it happened. What happened? I do not know exactly, and the details will remain, as far as I am concerned, one of the unsolved mysteries of my world. In those few seconds, a ski loomed up in front of me and I found myself incredulously wondering why the safety binding had not yet opened; the binding holds the ski boot firmly in position on the ski. My glasses were smashed. And my ankle was first twisted one way and then ripped the other. Instinctively, I tried to stand up; I heard a crack – and fell again. A thought flashed, 'Now you've really done it.' And I was right!

I lay in the snow, perhaps a little dazed, and noticed the red droplets around me in the virgin whiteness; then, I thought, I should at least sit up. My boots were still firmly held in the bindings; like any other average skier, I had fallen from time to time, and those bindings had opened without fail. Now my daughter was next to me. In a helpful, gentle way, she opened the bindings and released the safety straps. Now we could take stock of our suddenly new situation. Raising my right leg to test the strength in my ankle, I was reminded of lifting a solid, heavy lump of sirloin when bargain hunting in a supermarket a week previously. It was heavy, lifeless and apparently cold. The ankle was useless, and it was pointless to pretend otherwise.

While we were discussing our quickest approach to the ski patrol, a band of young people appeared above us. In turn, each stopped next to us on the narrow trail, gave us a quick glance – and sped on. I was obviously an obstacle which needed careful circumvention. Another young skier then studied me for several seconds and seemed to wonder if I had hurt myself. She was evidently not convinced; having satisfied her curiosity, she quickly disappeared from view.

Three thousand feet up on a windy afternoon and lying helplessly on a thinly covered patch of ice on a little–used trail, is not the most encouraging of situations. My daughter would have called the ski patrol, but she was not certain that she would again find our spot; so, we decided to stay together for the moment.

And then we received our most welcome visitor, an excellent skier who stopped in an instant and said little, but he had an expression on his face which said, 'I've seen this before'.

"Broken?" he asked.

"I don't know."

As he fleetingly left us, I heard the words, "I'll let them know."

Half an hour went by. We talked a little, agreed it was getting colder and, every couple of minutes, we glanced above us at the narrow, empty, darkening slope. As always, there was hope; but as time passed, it was not easy to avoid a feeling of apprehension and, perhaps, a trace of anxiety.

Then, hardly visible in the approaching darkness, a heavy–looking form appeared at the top of the slope.

The ski patrol had found us. Our instant friend had kept his word; he has the right to know that I shall feel eternally grateful.

Jim and Peter were physical opposites. Jim, who managed the stretcher, was tall, lanky and blue–eyed; Peter was short, compactly built and dark. But they worked in perfect unison. Chatting amiably, they asked me a few questions, and, within five minutes, the lower part of my leg was in a splint. After the other leg was secured to the injured one, they carried me gently onto the stretcher, wrapped me in blankets and firmly battened me down. After a brief enquiry about my comfort, Jim held the sledge boom and announced, "Now we are ready for the voyage."

The sledge began to move, initially slowly, over the hard–packed snow and ice. We were en route. My daughter would meet us later, at the bottom of the mountain.

The trip down was uneventful. At one stage, Jim suggested I should raise my head to see for myself a particularly tricky stretch, which had just been negotiated. I was full of admiration. As we reached the lower levels, we seemed to move faster. Now it was as though we were moving so rapidly that I wondered if my guardians were still there. Could I be travelling ever faster down the mountain, like a canoe caught in a quickening current? Lying on your back, firmly secured on a stretcher and with your head lower than your feet, is not a position in which you should permit the imagination to exploit a shocked personality. Suddenly, we were slowing down and the periodic enquiry after my comfort broke the relative silence. The reassuring figure of Peter appeared at my side; I noticed he was carrying my skis and poles.

Now we were down. The stretcher was manhandled into a hut and, while Jim asked me my name and other details, Peter carefully sponged off my face. The girl whom we had briefly seen in an accident at the top of the mountain was already in the hut and she seemed concerned about the blood on my face. I explained that it was superficial. But the ankle was another matter. Five minutes later, Jim and Peter were gently sliding me into an ambulance.

I thought of the promising beginning to that afternoon, of the lonely spot on the little–used, narrow trail, and of my daughter's levelheadedness. But above all, I thought of the ski patrol. How can you express your gratitude adequately? In circumstances such as these, I prefer the simple, 'Thank you for all your competence and kindness' approach. The response was equally simple, "It's nothing, sir; it's our duty."

With two broken bones and torn ligaments safely encased in plaster, using crutches, I returned on Monday morning to the world of business and bureaucracy. A friendly soul opined that, "You never really think it could actually happen to you, do you?"

After many years of skiing, I could only respond that I had never thought about an accident at all. Does a motorist think of a possible accident when he is en route? Does a pedestrian think he will be run over when he crosses the road? Does a pilot think of an impending air disaster with himself at the controls? God forbid! So why should the humble skier countenance an accident?

With hindsight, after an accident, you may blame yourself; you might conceivably blame others. But it is pointless to torment yourself with academic thoughts of this nature, because whatever the reason for the accident, you must come to terms with a fait accompli.

If your accident happens to occur on a ski mountain, be grateful for the ski patrol. Like a guardian angel, they will be there in your moment of need. From ordinary skiers like me, they will always have respect and gratitude. They will also receive an annual financial contribution. They are more than worth it.

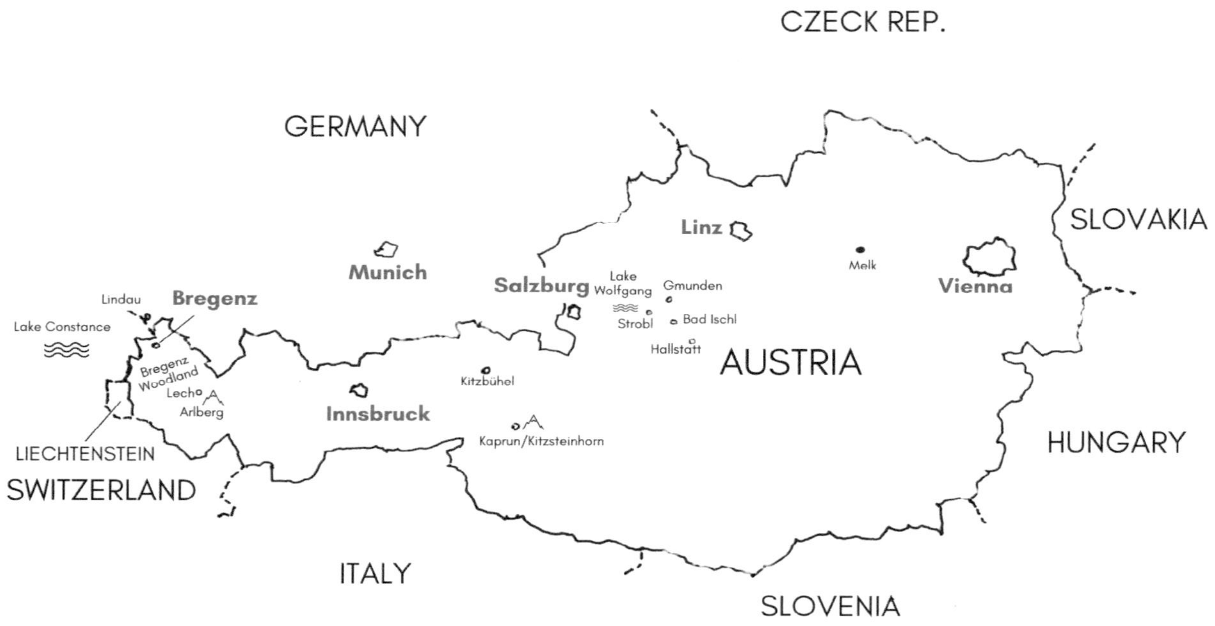

Austria – places detailed in the text, are shown on the map

TEN

MY WORLD – THE BEAUTY OF AUSTRIA

This story is about Austria, one of the most beautiful countries in the world. My introduction to Austria took place many years ago; I wanted to learn to ski. Travelling from London by train, I met my future wife. Emy was Austrian; however, she lived in London. There she had taken an honours degree in zoology. I was already working against locust plagues in the Horn of Africa; so, we had no lack of topics to discuss.

After my retirement, we decided to live in Vienna, which is known throughout the world as a beautiful city. Over the years, we travelled throughout Austria. Although Austria is normally categorised as a mountainous country, in fact, in its eastern part, the country is relatively flat, or somewhat gently undulating. The eastern part of Austria merges with the Hungarian Plains. Geographically, Austria and the United Kingdom have a number of similarities. Both countries are quite small; both have very beautiful landscapes. Both countries have a so–called Lake District, and both have scenic mountains, although, in general, the Austrian mountainous area is more extensive, and the mountains are higher. One could go on; for example, both countries possess charming little towns and villages; and both have many places of historical interest.

Melk Monastery

After living for a number of years in Austria, perhaps most of us can identify with a feeling that, from time to time, it might be pleasant to 'go away' for a few days. We shared the 'little nostalgia trip' feeling – why not journey into the Austrian countryside, just for a few days.

It was already late October when we set off one Saturday morning. Although a couple of weeks earlier, heavy snowfalls had been recorded in the mountains, now the weather had turned quite mild, with a yellowy sun occasionally casting a golden light over the landscape. Our destination was a charming little hotel (*Gasthof*) situated a few kilometres outside of Bad Ischl, which is a town close to the centre of Austria. The inn is called 'Gasthof zur Wacht' and an iron sentinel still remains to remind us that it was here that watch was maintained over the borders between the two provinces of Upper Austria and Salzburg, a city to the north.

We drove steadily along the West Motorway, a magnificent highway which links Vienna with the industrial city of Linz and beyond to Salzburg. Since we came to live in Austria, I have always been impressed that a country with such a small population (9 million) could not only construct a fine motorway system, but also maintain it in excellent condition, with the minimum of inconvenience to the users. Currently, Austria's motorway network extends to 1,750 kilometres. After initially driving through the glorious Vienna Woods, we continued along the motorway, enjoying the undulating fields (some planted with winter crops) and meadows, which stretched to the horizon. We have travelled this route many times, but it is never boring for a moment. And from time to time, one sees lovely monasteries, such as Melk.

The town of Melk is old and charming. However, Melk is famous throughout the world for its monastery, especially its abbey and ancient library, which contains thousands of handwritten books.

There are 36 monasteries in Austria. All are active, usually with well-maintained buildings; often, the monasteries own extensive vineyards, the sale of wine which is produced helping to meet the upkeep of the monasteries. Most monasteries offer an education through schooling; usually, one of the main subjects taught includes all aspects of agriculture.

Melk Abbey has been designated by UNESCO as a World Heritage Site. The monastery was founded by the Order of Benedictines in the 11th century. Closely associated with the monastery is its patron saint, who was called Coloman. It is said that Coloman was the son of the king of Ireland. He wished to avoid succeeding his father. Having taken his decision, in 1040, he intended to visit the Holy Land. When he reached Austria, he stayed in a small town near Vienna. Austria was under threat from other countries; probably because of this, its population tended to be nervous and suspicious.

The patron Saint of Melk, Saint Columar, from Ireland.

In any case, Coloman was suspected as a spy. He could not explain where he had come from, nor where he was going. After being questioned and tortured, he was hanged from the bough of a tree. When the truth of the situation eventually became clear, the Benedictine monks decided to honour the memory of Coloman by naming him as their Patron Saint in Melk.

The original monastery buildings were replaced in the first half of the 18th century, that was during the baroque period. These buildings are generally regarded as a masterpiece of baroque architecture. In front of the beautiful, towering façade of the church is a statue of Saint Coloman. The church has been built on rising ground; on one side, it overlooks the town of Melk and on the other side flows the River Danube. The river flows through a valley called the *Wachau*; this is a particularly beautiful stretch of twenty kilometres or so, characterized by steep hills with terraced vineyards.

Yes, Melk is indeed a gem which sparkles in so many ways.

Soon we were passing the industrial city of Linz (which incidentally has a charming old quarter). Now we were driving along the edge of Lake Traun and reached Gmunden, a lovely little town, well known for ceramic ware and pottery. Leaving Gmunden behind us, we passed through several quaint villages, each of them no doubt gems in summer; in fact, we were reminded a little of summer, as a few remaining flowers brightened the October day with the odd splash of colour. We reached Bad Ischl, a town in Austria's Lake District, in the afternoon. We parked in the town, not far from the fast–flowing River Traun. The river, quite noisily frothing here and there as the water flowed over stones or little rocks, runs through the centre of the town.

Bad Ischl is an interesting town. Like so many towns and cities around the world, it tends to fall into a pattern. Many years ago, Bad Ischl passed through a wave of development; however, now it has relapsed into sleepy serenity. Nowadays, the town relies mainly on Austrian visitors and tourism to support its economy.

Bad Ischl was part of the Hallstatt civilization which flourished in about 1,500B.C. Subsequently, it became a customs outpost of the Roman Empire. During the early centuries of Christendom, the general area which today is known as Bad Ischl was subject to the rule of various peoples, such as those of Bavaria to the west and Styria to the south.

In the eleventh century, the mining of salt was developed and expanded. In the following century, the area fell under the governance of the Habsburgs. The mining and marketing of salt remained the core of the town's economy; in fact, in 1656, the name *Salzkammergut* was first used officially, it described the town of Bad Ischl. *Salzkammergut* literally means 'The Estate of the Salt Chamber', the latter being the Habsburg Imperial Authority which managed and developed the valuable salt-mining industry. By the end of the 18th century, Bad Ischl was well established as an important centre of the salt industry. However, a much more glamorous future lay just around the corner, which ushered in the heyday of the town.

In 1807, a curious medical doctor investigated the properties of the saline water and started experiments to find out if the water had a healing effect on some of his patients. As these experiments progressed, in due course, another doctor (Dr. Franz Wirer) arrived to analyse the Bad Ischl water. A combination of these doctors' findings and conclusions resulted in both of them declaring that the water available in Bad Ischl could unquestionably be used to alleviate joint pains, as well as for general physical rehabilitation.

This led to Bad Ischl being named as a spa town. This was followed over the years by an expanding influx of guests who wished to take advantage of what the newly recognized spa had to offer. In turn, the increased number of visitors led to the construction not only of thermal baths, but also good quality hotels. The expansion of numbers of visitors began in earnest in the 1820s and continued unabated till the middle of the century. At this point, the town had achieved importance throughout Europe. Statesmen such as the then foreign minister of Austria, Prince Metternich, visited the spa regularly. The parents of the Emperor Franz Joseph (Franz Carl and Sophie), as well as Crown Prince Rudolf, were also guests of the town.

The high point of the incredibly successful heyday of Bad Ischl was the period 1849 to 1914. It was during this time that the town was named as the Emperor of Austria's summer residence. Little imagination is needed to see the picture of the royal family arriving for the summer, together with a considerable entourage of advisers and those whose job it was to maintain the comfort of the royal family. After all, during this period, Austria was the centre of a large and important empire. It was here that, in 1853, Franz Joseph and Elizabeth (Sissi) of Bavaria were betrothed, in preparation for marriage.

Over the years, many great European composers and artists stayed in Bad Ischl, among them the composer Anton Bruckner, who frequently played the organ for important festivities organized by the royal family. On the wall of the town's main church there is a memorial plaque to the great man. Anton Bruckner sojourned in Bad Ischl. It was also the favourite spa town of other composers, for example Johannes Brahms, Franz Lehar and Johann Strauss.

As more and more composers stayed in Bad Ischl (many of these composers were, or were, to become, famous internationally), the town gained its reputation as a highly important artistic centre of Europe. During this period, Bad Ischl was sometimes referred to as 'The Danube Monarchy'. Even today, operettas are performed in the main theatre throughout the summer. The theatre is situated close to the main part of the town and is surrounded by extensive, and lovely, gardens.

Having arrived in Bad Ischl, we walked through the town, passing the pastry and coffee house called Zauner. The firm was founded in Bad Ischl in 1832 and, during the period that the Habsburgs stayed in the town in their summer residence, Zauner was exclusively used as the imperial and royal purveyor to the court for their pastry products. In addition to the cafe in the town, Zauner has another establishment on the esplanade, by the river. Both cafes are elegant. They are much–frequented by the local population, as well as by visitors, like us.

With dusk approaching, we drove to the Gasthof zur Wacht, where we would spend the night. Outside of the town, we were soon passing the golf club. This brought back memories. Being a member of the Austrian Golf Seniors, for the tournament in Bad Ischl, our president had invited a world–famous golfer called José Maria Olazábal. On the first evening, as we were having dinner in a huge marquee, José Maria arrived. Our president introduced him, and invited him to say a few words. This is a part of what he said.

"Having just arrived from northern Spain, I especially enjoyed the drive from Salzburg to be with you here this evening. I would like to say how impressed I was with the most beautiful Austrian countryside. I have seen your mountains, your woodland, your meadows and your rushing streams. It was really all outstandingly beautiful. But let me add that there is always a danger that if you are surrounded by something beautiful, then eventually you may just take it for granted. Please do not let this happen. Beauty can never be taken for granted. It cannot look after itself. It needs to be protected, nourished and carefully looked after and loved. Please look after your beauty – I am sure it is unique."

A perceptive man indeed! And he was so right! After our dinner, we talked to José Maria, a charming man.

Arriving at the hotel, we were welcomed by the owner. Alfred is a big man, and he is always full of good cheer. Every evening, he sits with his 'regulars' while they all consume what seems to be a considerable volume of beer. For two or three hours each evening, the group of beer-drinkers exchange stories and jokes with one another – all the time drinking beer.

Because we wanted to leave at about 9 on the following day, we decided to attend the evening church service in Strobl, a village situated on the St. Wolfgang Lake, about 5 kilometres from our Gasthof. Strobl is an elegant little town and, in the 1800s, was home during the summer months to the aristocracy, many of whom had connections with the court. The late baroque church is named after a Saint Sigismund. Simple in its design, it is a typical Austrian country church, complete with its 'onion tower'. The priest was assisted by 10 servers, young boys wearing emerald–green cassocks. The congregation sang with piety. It was a lovely experience. The short journey back to the Gasthof was memorable because of the blackness outside; although it was about 7 in the evening, it seemed like the dead of night.

As we were leaving Strobl, I was reminded of a visit to the area by Chancellor Helmut Kohl. We understood that he was there to lose weight. I recalled that on that lovely summer's afternoon, he spoke informally to a small crowd for well over an hour. The atmosphere was totally relaxed, with no sign whatsoever of any form of security. Apart from thanking the inhabitants for their hospitality, he shared his vision of Europe's future with us. He spoke as though he was thinking aloud. We were all spellbound by the wealth of knowledge of this great statesman.

After he had finished and the prolonged applause had died down, we were offered coffee, cakes and cream. I had the feeling that Helmut Kohl may have eaten a little above his allowance! After a little more friendly chatting, Helmut Kohl was driven away, apparently to his hotel in nearby St. Gilgen.

After an early night at the Gasthof zur Wacht, next morning, we woke a little early by our normal standards. We went down to breakfast and looked outside. There before us was the sheer beauty of Austria. The Gasthof lies below some rocky hills; these are, in fact, the foothills of the Dachstein Massif, an extensive area of mountains which rise to 3,000 metres. The sun had risen over the mountains behind us, and the sun's rays were shining directly onto the meadows and the mountains which rose up behind them. The mountains were densely carpeted with fir trees, and they stood out as though on a predominantly deep-green canvas against the blue of the heavens behind. If a small cloud briefly impeded the sun's rays, then the green of the trees became a little darker.

But it was time to depart. We drove through this enchanting scenery towards Salzburg, passing the St. Wolfgang Lake, surrounded as it was by lovely mountains; sometimes we could see a bare rockface which seemed to slide directly into the glassy water. Across the lake, we could see the village of St. Wolfgang, bathed in sunshine. Next to the tower of the village church (famous for its magnificently carved altar) was the White Horse Inn. This brought back memories of our stays there, which were always enjoyable. Soon after, we drove through Fuschl, a beautiful little resort. Now we were approaching Salzburg, passing the pilgrimage church of Maria Plain, which is perched on a hill. The original chapel was constructed in 1632; however, due to the increasing numbers of pilgrims who came to the chapel, the church as we know it today was built.

Soon afterwards, we were passing Salzburg Castle, certainly one of the main attractions of the city. There are forty castles in Austria. Salzburg Castle was built high up on a rocky hill; it was built by Archbishop Gebhard in 1077. It replaced various fortifications which had been constructed over the millennia, including a fortress built by the Romans. Salzburg Castle is the largest in central Europe.

Now we were leaving Salzburg behind, and we were continuing westward towards Munich. Soon, the mountains gave way to flat, arable land and meadows, with Friesian and what looked like Hereford cattle. The German farmers apparently take great pride in their land, which is neatly cultivated in rich–looking soil and stretches into the distance; from time to time, we saw extensive farmsteads. It was a scene of total orderliness and peace.

Our progress towards Munich was steady and the driving was made easier due to the rule in Germany, and Austria, which forbids heavy traffic on the motorway between noon on Saturday and Sunday evening.

At about noon, we entered the outskirts of Munich, the capital city of Bavaria. With a population of 1.6 million, Munich is the third largest city in Germany, after Berlin and Hamburg. Our progress through the city was remarkably swift.

The centre of Munich is really the cathedral, an edifice dedicated to Our Blessed Lady the Virgin Mary. Munich was founded by Benedictine monks in the middle of the twelfth century. The name '*Muenchen*' is derived from '*Moenche*' – Monks. The cathedral replaced a Romanesque (Norman) church. The cathedral was commissioned by Duke Sigismund, with the construction beginning in 1468. The main part of the church was built in the late-Gothic style and has the capacity to house a standing congregation of 20,000. However, the two towers were not completed until about 50 years later; these reflect more the style of the Renaissance period, although there was also some foreign architectural influence. The towers, topped by domes, were modelled on those of the Dome of the Rock church in

Jerusalem, the latter reflecting late Byzantine architecture. The sheer size of the cathedral would always be imposing. In fact, its prominence is enhanced due to a law of the city which enforces a height limit on buildings; this results in the cathedral being seen from afar. The cathedral was severely damaged during WW2 – the roof collapsed. A great deal of restoration has been undertaken, with the last stage completed in 1994.

Now we would soon be leaving Munich behind. We continued westwards, but soon took the road in a southerly direction, which would lead us to Lindau, which is a German town close to the border with Austria. Both Lindau and the Austrian city of Bregenz are situated on Lake Constance. The distance from Munich to Bregenz is about 180 kilometres.

Lindau is an interesting town, with about 25,000 inhabitants. The old town was limited to an island, which was fortified. Lindau was first mentioned in history when an Irish monk, journeying from St. Gallen in Switzerland, spent some time there in 882. The parish church dates from 1180 and, in 1224, the Franciscans established a monastery there. In the 1500s, Lindau suffered dreadfully from the plague, which claimed numerous lives. Later, during the Thirty Years War, the Swedes laid siege to Lindau, in 1647. Lindau successfully defended itself and eventually broke the siege. You may agree with me, dear Reader, that it is interesting that one can find gems of history and culture in quiet corners of the world.

Soon, we crossed the border and entered Bregenz, the main city of Austria's most westerly province, which is called Vorarlberg. As I have described, Bregenz has been built along the shore of Lake Constance. Lake Constance covers an area of five thousand square kilometres and, in addition to Austria, its shores border Germany, Switzerland and Italy.

In the winter, Bregenz is a quiet, somewhat sleepy, city. But in summer, it can be overwhelmed with tourists. One of a number of attractions is The Bregenz Drama Festival, mainly a festival for theatre and opera. Each year, at least one opera is presented, using the stage which floats in Lake Constance. The stage is the largest in the world; the audience, which numbers five to six thousand, revels in the whole scene of magnificent opera productions, with Lake Constance as a wonderful backdrop.

From a commercial point of view, Bregenz and its outskirts can claim a series of success stories. For instance, in the summer months, at least one opera is presented; the tickers for the productions are usually quickly sold. The annual overall attendance is at least 200,000. Apart from tourist and cultural attractions, Bregenz (and its environs) has a strong design and manufacturing base. Part of the reason for this is the fact that, during the Cold War period from the middle to almost the end of the twentieth century, eastern Austria was virtually a cul de sac as far as commerce was concerned. The Iron Curtain effectively closed the Austrian border with Hungary, as well as with the then Czechoslovakia. To the south lay the Balkans. Given these circumstances, industrial activities which might normally have been established in eastern Austria were instead located in western Austria. There, one could trade with, and through, Switzerland, Italy and Germany, all three countries being in close proximity.

The firm Doppelmayr is located closely to the city; it is the largest and most successful manufacturer in the world of ski lifts and associated systems, such as rapid transit systems.

Close-by Dornbirn (a former centre for textiles) has reinvented itself with a large-scale trade fair, which attracts many thousands of visitors virtually throughout the year. One could go on with this story of imaginative development and the constant pursuit of new business initiatives.

Now we were on the last leg of the day's journey. We drove from Bregenz up into the hills and mountains of an area called The Bregenz Woodland. The large stretch of woods and forests stretch over a beautiful landscape of hills and mountains. The average altitude of The Bregenz Woodland is 1,000 metres above sea level.

Among its activities, Austrians and tourists enjoy beautiful walks. Industrially, logging is undertaken on a large scale. Hydroelectricity is under constant development. And the production of cheese certainly deserves a mention; in fact, one can follow the 'Cheese Route' and enjoy a good variety of cheeses which are particular to the region.

After a wonderfully interesting day, it was time to drive to a village called Hittisau, a picturesque village situated in the heart of The Bregenz Woodland. Apart from the road, which twists and turns as one gains altitude, the drive is lovely with pastures and conifer forest close to the road. In the distance, one sees the shining glaciers of the Swiss Alps. It would take about a half hour or so to reach Hittisau. We were soon installed in an hotel where we had stayed from time to time; the hotel is called The Crown. As always, we enjoyed our stay; a jewel in the hotel's delights is the cooking, which is of world standard.

Next day was the annual Austrian National Day, 26th October. Considering that there would be a reduced traffic density on the Austrian road system, with virtually no trucks at all, we decided to drive back to Vienna, using the southerly route, stopping overnight in Kitzbuehel, a lovely town known throughout the world as a skiing Mecca. With a journey of about

This is Austria

only 370 kilometres, we left in the late morning. We passed Feldkirch and Bludenz, before we began the climb towards the Arlberg Massif. Soon we reached Stuben, where there is a turn–off to a well–known skiing resort called Lech.

As we approached the Arlberg–mountain area, we noticed that the weather was becoming more overcast; however, it was not snowing. I had considered driving over the Arlberg on the magnificent mountain road which, at its highest point, ascends to 1,800 metres. However, as we approached the huge mountain, it soon became evident that, on this occasion, to take the mountain road would be foolhardy. Ahead of us was a dark-grey, dense curtain of mist and fog. Our alternative was to use the Arlberg tunnel, which we did – I might add, with thanks!

The Arlberg tunnel represents one of the greatest engineering successes of the last century. Built between mid 1974 and 1978, the tunnel is 14 kilometres long. With an elevation variant of 1,000 metres, it enables traffic to travel swiftly and safely (the illumination is perfect) through the Arlberg Massif, which at its highest elevation towers over the surrounding mountains at 2,800 metres (about 9,000 feet). The tunnel is designed for a capacity of 1,200 trucks per hour. The cost of the incredible construction, in the seventies, was 300 million euros; today's equivalent would be well over a billion euros.

The tunnel, which has stood the test of time in its operation, has a number of interesting characteristics. For instance, there are 45 closed circuit TV cameras in permanent operation to monitor the traffic flow. The tunnel is noteworthy for its highly effective ventilation system. There are 4 ventilation centres, each operating and controlling a system of ventilation shafts; one of these is 736 metres deep (the deepest in Europe). On average, the tunnel is used by about three million vehicles each year.

When we emerged from the tunnel, we found a weather change; the sky was clear and the snow on the surrounding mountains looked gorgeous against the azure. After a brief stop to take in the wonderful scenery, we continued towards Innsbruck, the main city of Tirol. En route we passed through a number of additional tunnels, varying in length between one and five kilometres. Between the tunnels, we wondered at the most beautiful mountains, each partly clothed in carpets of forest, mainly conifers. Below were rushing, frothing torrents of small rivers or streams, the sparkling water fed from the snows. Sometimes, as we looked skywards, we could see brilliant-white waterfalls tumbling down a mountain rock face. After passing the entrance of a broad valley, where we once explored the glorious mountains, we passed Innsbruck.

Innsbruck, like Linz, has a lovely old quarter. It has fine churches, one or two of which date from the 15th century. Perhaps the most famous feature of the old town is the Golden Roof. Historically, it is said that the Golden Roof was constructed during a siege by the French. When the besiegers saw the Golden Roof being constructed, they concluded that the Austrians had plenty of resources, not only to survive, but the Austrians might well repel the siege; so, the besiegers lifted the siege.

The Golden Roof was constructed in the early part of the 15th century as a part of the residence of the Austrian Emperor Maximilian I. As an interesting detail, his first wife was Maria of Burgundy. His second wife was Bianca Maria Sforza of Milan. On the occasion of his second marriage, in a gesture aimed at preventing the alienation of allies and important friends, whom had been gained through his first marriage, he had himself painted on his balcony standing between the two women.

We arrived in Kitzbuehel just before dusk. Our hotel was a delight. Over the years, we have stayed in many hotels around the world. One's judgement of an hotel is inevitably subjective. For some, to be picked up on arrival at the airport in Hong Kong and driven to the Peninsula Hotel in one of the hotel's fleet of Rolls Royce limousines might represent the ultimate. Or to stay at the Royal Orchid Sheraton, or the Oriental (of Somerset Maugham fame) in Bangkok might also, justifiably, be regarded as hospitality par excellence. Suffice it to say that, for me at least, when I stay at the Hotel zur Tenne in Kitzbuehel, I always come away with the feeling, 'What else could one possibly want in a thoroughly excellent hotel?'

So, what is to be enjoyed in the Hotel zur Tenne? First, although the hotel is situated in the main street of Kitzbuehel, it is nevertheless quiet. Next, from the reception to the chamber maids, and at all levels of staff in–between, one meets quiet competence and courtesy. Then there is the question of functionality. Everything functions perfectly. But for me, this is not enough – a good hotel has to have charm and a warm atmosphere. The Tenne has this to a degree. Throughout, the decor is Tirolean, with beamed ceilings and generously warm furnishings. Our bedroom was large, with a lovely bay window, which enabled us to look out over the picturesque main street of Kitzbuehel, with its houses painted in various lovely colours. Our room offered us a king–sized bed, spacious cupboards, easy chairs and, in the corner, upholstered seats around a quite large, rustic table. The bathroom was tiled and clean. Could one reasonably ask for more? We were living in unassuming, quiet luxury. And there was a refreshing lack of exaggeration, or 'pomp and circumstance'. For me, the Hotel zur Tenne is a delight!

Our final day of driving around Austria started with a perfect, and generous, breakfast at the hotel, served in the light, airy and spacious breakfast room. Soon it would be time to leave. Our car was parked (with a special hotel pass) outside the hotel front door and we departed from Kitzbuehel at about 10 o'clock. We felt wonderfully relaxed; in beautiful sunshine, we glided through meadows and woodland, sometimes passing over little bridges; below, were bubbling streams. This was a drive of about two hours. The constantly changing light seemed to cast a spell of beauty over our surroundings. The delicate rays of the October sun filtered ever so gently through the autumnal leaves of the woods. Sometimes, we would pass a wall of rock as we skirted a mountain–face; suddenly, we would be cast into the gloom of deep shadow. Then, quite suddenly, the sun would be bathing the countryside in glorious sunshine.

Yes, this was Austria at its most beautiful best. Once we reached the highway, we felt that this was the 'home stretch' – and so it was. Now we were home – and we would continue living in Vienna, our idyllic city.

This book is printed on paper from sustainable sources managed under the Forest Stewardship Council (FSC) scheme.

It has been printed in the UK to reduce transportation miles and their impact upon the environment.

For every new title that Troubador publishes, we plant a tree to offset CO_2, partnering with the More Trees scheme.

MORE TREES
LET'S PLANT A BILLION TREES

For more about how Troubador offsets its environmental impact, see www.troubador.co.uk/sustainability-and-community